Montreal Confidential

~

Our Old Man used to always say that you can take the boy out of Montreal but you can't take Montreal out of the boy.

Some cities are merely blots on the landscape with the approved collection of steel and stone buildings and the ever-present supermarkets. Most have absolutely nothing to distinguish them from a thousand similar cities.

Some, notably New York, New Orleans and San Francisco, have certain characteristics which set them apart from the other cities.

And then there's Montreal.

There is little doubt but that our home town has developed into the most colorful community on the continent. Nothing which New York, New Orleans or San Francisco—or any other city for that matter—can offer that Montreal hasn't more of.

It is a helluva town to visit, a helluva town to live in and a helluva town to come back to. We love every grimy square foot of it.

AL PALMER

Montreal Confidential

Al Palmer

Véhicule Press

Published with the generous assistance of the Book
Publishing Industry Development Program of the Department of Canadian Heritage and the Société de dévelop-
pement des entreprises culturelles du Québec (SODEC).

Cover design: David Drummond
Special assistance: Rosemary Dardick
Frontispiece: Concordia University Archives
Front and back cover images: Concordia University Archives
Set in Minion and Imprint MT Shadow by Simon Garamond
Printed by Marquis Printing Inc.

LIBRARY AND ARCHIVES CANADA CATALOGUING
IN PUBLICATION
Palmer, Al
Montreal confidential / Al Palmer ; foreword by
William Weintraub.
Originally published in 1950.
Includes index.
ISBN 978-1-55065-260-4
1. Montréal (Québec)—Social life and customs—
20th century.
2. Montréal (Québec)—Description and travel. I. Title.
FC2947.394.P3 2009   971.4'2804   C2009-903484-0

Published by Véhicule Press, Montréal, Québec, Canada
www.vehiculepress.com

Distribution in Canada by LitDistCo
www.litdistco.ca

Distributed in the U.S. by Independent Publishers Group
www.ipgbook.com

Printed in Canada on recycled paper

Contents

Publisher's Note (2009)

This is a reincarnation of Al Palmer's long out-of-print *Montreal Confidential* which was published in September 1950 as a News Stand Library Pocket Edition. To contribute to the reader's appreciation of Montreal's night life during Palmer's time, we have taken the liberty of illusrating this edition with photographs of people and places mentioned in the book. Most images have been gleaned from the Concordia University Archives. Typos that appeared in the original book have been corrected; however, certain negative attitudes of the period towards various groups remain.

An Appreciation
William Weintraub

BACK IN THOSE DAYS, in the late 1940s, I used to look at Al Palmer with awe and envy. Al Palmer was a star—a journalist with a column, a friend of celebrities, a man who knew all of Montreal's secrets. I, by contrast, was a too-young cub reporter who knew nothing.

At Slitkin and Slotkin's restaurant, the newspapermen's hangout on Dorchester Street, Al Palmer would sit at one of the important tables, at the back, sipping an expensive rum and coke. Meanwhile I would be nursing my humble quart of Black Horse Ale, sitting at one of the up-front tables reserved for the peasantry. Al, as always, would be resplendent in a made-to-measure suit, and with him would be a gorgeous blonde, probably a chorus girl from one of the nearby nightclubs. With me, at my table, would be two fellow *Gazette* reporters, underpaid wretches with ketchup stains on their neckties.

When Al Palmer's long-awaited book, *Montreal Confidential,* finally came out in 1950, I immediately bought a copy. It promised "The Low Down on the Big Town" and that was exactly what I needed. Montreal was celebrated in those days as a wide-open town, but you still had to know the ropes. For instance it was strictly forbidden to smuggle a woman into your hotel room, with hotel detectives always on the alert, but Al's book told you how to do it (see page 134).

The book was full of useful advice, like how to impress the lady on your first date (if you were "loaded with loot"). You should start with cocktails at the swanky Indian Room on St. Catherine Street, after which you should taxi up to the Sunset Strip for dinner at the fashionable Ruby Foo's. Then downtown again, to take in the show at the Bellevue Casino or the Folies Bergères or both. Your date might be hungry again by then, so you ought to repair to the Chic-N-Coop for spareribs. From there—it's well after midnight now—it's only a two-minute walk to Ciro's, where you can "let the chick get her kicks to some of the finest jive available in town." If the "chick" were ever to become your steady girlfriend, Al advises that will she will expect to be taken out on Tuesdays, Thursdays and Saturdays—the "Sweetheart Nights" in Montreal.

In his excellent *vade mecum*, Al Palmer takes us to a dozen glamorous nightclubs, but he doesn't neglect the seamy side of the city. He takes us to the corner of St. Catherine Street and St. Lawrence, where "you'll find the riff raff of the world scurrying around like wharf rats." Farther down St. Lawrence there are flop houses where you can get a bed for the night, to share with bedbugs, for twenty-five cents. And down at Craig Street there's Skid Row, where the rubby-dubs stagger around. The favorite drink of these tattered unfortunates is rubbing alcohol flavored with vanilla extract.

In this part of town, Al tells us, "it is rough, tough, lusty and lewd," but he still insists on Montreal's virtues. Here, during a night on the town, he says, you're less likely to be rolled than in any other major city. And this town, unlike others, is not plagued by zoot suiters. (If you don't know what getting rolled means, or what zoot suiters are, ask your grandfather.)

In this book, Montreal is very much an English-speaking city. Al Palmer acknowledges that Francophones outnumber Anglophones by far, but he pays little attention to them. He notes that there is very little friction between the two communities, although he admits that it's much easier to get along in the city if you speak French. But, he laments, very few Anglos take the trouble to learn the language. For the year 1950, when the book came out, this was a fair assessment of the situation.

One of the reasons for Al Palmer's Anglocentrism was that his world was the world of show business, and almost all the performers for nightclubs and theaters were Americans, engaged through New York booking agencies. The flavor of entertainment, the songs and the comedy, were strictly American. The Montreal-New York axis was a strong one, and the *New York Daily News* was a big seller at newsstands here. Even this book of Al's, *Montreal Confidential*, was inspired by a book called *New York Confidential*, which came out two years earlier.

In the New York book, a lady frequently seen in night-clubs is a "doll-about-town," and Al Palmer seems to have picked up much of this Broadway lingo. Al is not content to simply talk about attractive women walking down the Street; for him they are "local lovelies ankling along." If you have lots of money you have "heavy cabbage." If Al can't find a known slang term that suits him, he invents one. Thus ladies of easy virtue are "trampettes." Beer is "stupor suds" and liquor is "stagger syrup." The recent

World War II was the "Late Hate."

Al's frisky, inventive prose is always in honor of his main theme—his affection for Montreal. "It's not so much a city as a state of mind," he writes. "To live there is to love it. Those of us who were fortunate enough to be born there consider it the nearest approach to Heaven we know of without leaving the ground."

By unearthing this long-buried book, this treasure of Al Palmer's, Simon Dardick, Nancy Marrelli and their Véhicule Press have made a fine and original contribution to our understanding of the history of Montreal.

Montreal, 2009

For Eddie Quinn,
the noblest Hibernian

Forward (Very)

MONTREAL WAS FOUNDED on the 18th day of May, 1692, by the Sieur de Maisonneuve, who probably had no idea of what he was starting. So far the city has had three names: Hochelaga, Ville Marie and Montreal. The latter is a musical take-off on Mont Real, the name given that hunk of vegetation which juts up like an outsized falsie in the north-central section of the town.

English-speaking residents call it "Mawn-tree-all"; French-Canadians call it "Morry-All"; Americans call is "MUN-tree-all"; and envious Torontonians, frustrated by the bluest blue laws in the country, call it several names, none of which will be mentioned here.

Montreal boasts of a population of approximately a million souls—some about which she doesn't boast too loudly. During the years when the United States was scrapping with Mother England for her independence, the city was invaded by American forces. Today the town is still being invaded by Americans but they now carry huge wads of Yankee dollars instead of whatever the plural of blunderbuss happens to be.

The town is loaded with historical interest. Seems as though you can't walk two blocks without bumping into a plaque or a monument describing this battle or praising that adventurous gent or the usual "on this site stood" sort of thing.

The population is predominately French, with English-speaking races running a rather slow second. The two races live side by side in perfect harmony, except on rare occasions when some professional do-gooder (usually from a different province) comes in to stick his meddlesome hands into what is strictly a Quebec affair.

Camillien Houde, the perennial mayor, spent most of the war years in a concentration camp. He was released a few months before his re-election to office. Like the perennial premier, Maurice Duplessis, he is a popular figure. Both men appear to have wiped out any serious competition for their respective offices with their sheer force of popularity. It may be well to note at this time that both have huge English-speaking support—which is the way it should be in a bilingual province.

Montreal's early struggles included the approved battles with the Redskins; the usual plagues, fires, riots, depressions, etc., none of which will be mentioned here. If you are looking for a historical guide to Montreal … brother, have you got the wrong book!

First-time visitors to Montreal are impressed by the number of places in which you can get stiff as board and by the love affair each Montrealer is carrying on with his home town. True, citizens of New York, Paris, New Orleans and San Francisco are famous for the affection they hold for their cities, but Montrealers make a career of it.

This book is by no means intended as an official Baedeker to Montreal. It doesn't tell you how to find a hotel room and a companion—if you're under 21 we wouldn't tell you and if you're over 21 you shouldn't need to be told. Nor will you learn from this book how to interpret what the streetcar conductor is saying—it's our home town and we don't know either.

This book is merely a collection of legends, facts, after-dark data, and gleanings from the memories of guys and gals who were around when it happened. For most of the chapters we are indebted to the following:

Yvon Robert, Maurice Robert, Lou Wyman, Jack Rogers, Tiny and Betty Koren, Ben Cossman, Pearl Fields, The Freres Orlando, Lili St. Cyr, Gino Lombard, Eddie the bartender at Folies Bergères, Bob the headwaiter at the same spot, Elmer Ferguson, Marcel the busboy at Slitkins and Slotkins, Bob the colored boy in the washroom at La Bohème, his colleague at the Bellevue Casino, Harry Holmock, Phil Lipsen, Tony the Tailor, Maestro Peter Barry, Jerry (The Host) Taylor, half of the bellboy staff at the Laurentien Hotel, three-quarters of the waiters at the same beloved inn, many and varied cab drivers, Pax Plante, a couple of members of the Detective Bureau, Harold Gardner, Bruce Taylor, Freddie Roberts, Jasmine Rheaume, Emile Viens, Frank the waiter at the Copa, Majou the Brazilian chorine, Fernand and Jules Racicot, Andy Monette, the Hill Brothers, the tray-toters at the Chick-N-Coop, the staff at the Indian Room, Rudy, Bob, and the other mixologists too numerous to list, Johnny Howard (if you'll pardon the expression), Alan Gale, Buddy Clarke, Frank Fuoco—the Noble Roman, Fitz, Sam Vineberg, Arthur Schalek, Gus Garber and a stray electrical supply man we met one morning at Hi-Ho Café.

And, of course, Pat Gale, Harry Luce, Harry Smith, Tony, Mike and George Dmitri, Johnny Gardner, Oscar

Peterson, Albert "Abdul" Lean, Billy Kotsos, Peter "Pop" Kotsonas, Dave Bier, Dave Greenbery, Tommy Tomasso, Henry Manella, Michel Normandin, Hal Stubbs, Roy Castleman, Bob Harvie, an unidentified lush we met at an east-end oyster bar, Frank D'Asti, Freddie the Count, Louie the Lawyer, Kid Ohblay, Jockey Fleming, Butch Obie, Rocky Goldberg, Hickey the Lightman, a horse player out of Baltimore, Al Rodney, and Roy Cooper.

Cherchez La Femme

BACK IN THE DAYS when Montreal was still sporting a three-cornered sarong, Jean Talon, a solid citizen of New France, if there ever was one, gave the town's vital statistics a long, hard look and discovered that the male population far outnumbered that of the female of the species.

Apart from the fact that male immigration exceeded the female figure, the Carignan Regiment, brought to this country to make the Indians say the Iroquois equivalent of "uncle" were very reluctant to return home.

Ranks of eligible males were also swelled by thousands of coureurs-de-bois who spent most of their waking hours screaming and shrieking through the forest and generally acting like the savages they were.

Talon was greatly perturbed over this sorry state of affairs and hurriedly pulled some trans-Atlantic political strings. In less time than it takes to say "Vive la France" groups of demure damsels were gathered up in the Old Country and placed aboard ships for Quebec.

These were no ordinary dolls. They were highly-screened, very eligible maidens who bore the distinctive title of "Filles de Roi," King's girls.

The arrival of the first shipload at Quebec was greeted with great celebration. The scene incidentally is depicted in the north wall of the Men's Press Club in the Laurentien Hotel. It is the work of the famed Montreal artist LaPalme and will give you a fairly good idea of how enthusiastic was the welcome given to the chicks. Yet.

Eligible bachelors were ordered to marry within fifteen days of the arrival of a shipload of these gals—depending, of course, upon the available supply.

Bachelors (guys who never make the same mistake once) who refused to wed were given a hard time by the government. They were not permitted to trade with the savages or to hunt. They were forbidden to whoop it up with local Hiawathas—they couldn't even go fishing.

Faced with these hardships, a few accepted the alternative. The majority, however, eagerly donned double harness and strains of the Lohengrin Lockstep were heard all over the place. As many as thirty marriages were performed in one fell swoop—although this seems like pretty small potatoes today when one remembers a few years back when the ball park was used as the setting of the greatest number of mass marriages ever performed.

As soon as the ready, able and willing was welded to his ever-loving King's girl, the government kicked in with eleven crowns in money, a cow, an ox, two barrels of salted meat, a pair of swine and a pair of fowls. True, a lot of guys today do better than that, but this was centuries ago when eleven crowns was a lot of cabbage indeed.

In this way the government urged by Jean Talon, relieved the first female famine in the history of the town. There hasn't been a serious shortage since.

But if you think you can walk along St. Kit's [St. Catherine Street] and choose any of the local lovelies ankling along there, we have news for you. Montreal maidens are notably stand-offish when accosted on the streets and have a habit of calling a copper if approached by strange men.

The same applies to those sitting *en seul* in bars. It is not a rare sight to see a little bit of fluff all alone on a bar stool. She may be the girl friend, or wife of a waiter or cab driver waiting for her mate to get off duty. Should this be the case, you had better forget the possibility of engaging her in light conversation—or you may wake up with a broken head instead of that one night of love you envisioned.

If you also think you can visit the widely-publicized Red Light district, and walk cheerfully into an elaborate brothel—you're living in the past, son. The Red Light district is closed tighter than a Toronto cocktail bar on Sunday.

Time was when the area, including such streets as St. Dominique, Clark, Charlotte Lane, Cadieux (now de Bullion), Lagauchetière, Mayor, Hôtel de Ville and Berger was world-famous as a wide-open flesh spot. Today the area is inhabited mostly by European families who work nine to five and who are liable to boot you down the stairs if you ask if Annie lives there anymore.

During the Late Hate, the Army accomplished what decades of policing failed to do. It closed up the district and put many hundreds of filles de joie out of work. Today the numerals "312" are only used by night club comics when they know there are old-timers in the house.

At one time, the number adorned the door of a well-known bordello on Ontario Street, operated by a colorful character known as Madame Bobbe. Her nearest rival was a well-padded matron who ran a similar place on Mayor Street. The latter spot gained considerable publicity in pre-war days following one of its many raids. With a red-sealed padlock on its portals, the house advertised "Business as usual next door." This little example of business promotion irked the City Hall considerably.

Other well-known spots included Maggie's on Clark Street which gained fame among newspapermen when one of their members stole—on a five dollar bet—the ornate hat tree which occupied a prominent place in the hallway. Maggie chased the culprit through the snow to the corner of St. Kit's [St. Catherine]where a curious cop collared the fugitive. All was forgiven, however, and the madame and the scribe—and the cop—returned to her establishment where much beer was consumed by all and sundry.

With their happy hunting grounds closed to them, the trampettes spread all over the city. A few years ago, several of the more industrious set up a call house system operating out of a Milton Street apartment. In no time whatsoever the arm of the law reached into the joint and collared the madame and a book listing some of the most prominent men in the city. That was the last attempt at anything like organized prostitution on a high scale.

Frustrated and forlorn, the tramp today haunts the lower type bars and cafes. She has degenerated to the hooker class. If you get the right taxi driver he may fix you up on the old "ten and three" basis. Ten for the doll and three for the room—which, in most cases, will turn out to be a sordid tourist house on an equally sordid side street.

The one bright note in this sorry state of affairs is that you are less likely to be rolled in Montreal than in any other major city. The tramps are necessarily honest and fear the Morality Squad. If you get rolled, be a smart guy—call a cop.

Don't try to pick up a gal on the street. Don't try to date one in a night club without first consulting your waiter. If you want any more advice than this—read Dr. Kinsey's Report.

The End of an Era

MONTREAL'S UNDERWORLD lost its major league status on a pleasant July afternoon in 1946, when Louis Bercovitch, better known as Joe Miller, filled "edge man" Harry Davis full of uncomfortable bullet holes in the latter's horse parlor on Stanley Street. Elmer Ferguson, of *The Herald*, the dean of Canadian sports writers, described the incident as being one of Joe Miller's unfunnier jokes.

The aging, graying Davis had recently been released from penitentiary after serving a lengthy term on a narcotic rap. He got back into action in time to inherit the "edge" from the late Arthur Davidson. The "edge" is strictly a Montreal term used to signify the go-between for gamblers, politicians and police. Holder of the "edge" is undisputed boss of all vice in the city and has the final say-so in all matters concerning gambling and other less reputable endeavors.

To operate any type of sub-rosa business in the city it is, or rather was, necessary to first receive the sanction of the "edge" who notified all concerned that the green light had been granted or had not been granted, depending largely on your connections.

If the official nod was not forthcoming your establishment was closed post haste and all you reaped from your venture was experience. If you were among the favored few upon whom the "edge" smiled you were in business. It was as simple as that.

Since Davis racked up his cue and went to Paperman's there has been no "edge" in Montreal. Anyone so daring as to open a gambling spot or a bordello in the city will find the place lousy with cops in less time than it takes to say "Concordia Salus."

Although it is generally believed that "uneasy lies the head that wears the edge," Davis was the only one to die a violent death. Eddie Baker and Arthur Davidson, who succeeded him, died peacefully in bed. There has been no official "edge" man in the town since 1946.

The murder of Harry Davis jolted the country. Complacent citizens who lived in an "it can't happen here" state of mind realized, probably for the first time, that Montreal's gangdom was a real and vicious thing.

Countless tons of printer's ink has been used describing the events between Davis' murder and the ultimate surrender of Joe Miller. Endless tonsils have been strained relating fanciful versions of Ted McCormick's journalistic scoop over the airways. No one, however, has had the story straight. Herewith, therefore, is the true picture for the first time.

Immediately following the killing, Miller circulated in the uptown area, shifting from phone booth to phone booth in an attempt to locate Ted McCormick, then managing editor of *The Herald*, who also wrote a column under the by-line of Sean Edwin.

Miller figured he would get a better deal with the law if he were to get to McCormick first and tell his story before surrendering.

This writer, then a reporter at *The Herald*, checked in for duty late that afternoon to find the city room deserted except for Stan Cornthwaite, then city editor, who briefed us on the known facts of the killing and told us of Miller's frequent phone calls.

Miller was now calling every three minutes from various parts of the city. The phone calls went on for the space of an hour and a half before McCormick, carrying two of Davis' bloodstained cigars, returned to the paper and took a call from the fugitive.

After a short conversation with Miller, McCormick told us to find a room and to stand by for further instructions. He then left to keep an appointment with Miller and a friend of the latter's.

Faced with the problem of finding a room in which a rendezvous may be held with a known killer, this writer aged four years. The town was bristling with guns. Every available policeman had been called to duty and every mobster in town was on the march. Our room at the Ford hotel was out of the question. We knew it would be suicide to bring Miller there. After all, who wants to sidle up to the bull's eye during a night when target practice seemed to be the order of things?

Fortunately, a relative of ours had gone to the country, leaving the key to their flat in Verdun in our keeping. True, they hadn't left instructions to harbor fugitives in their pleasant home—but then again, they hadn't specifically ordered otherwise.

McCormick's instructions were to join Buster Arless, of the famed photographic family, and to drive to an alleyway off Prince Arthur Street.

It was early dusk when Arless parked his black sedan in an appointed place and yours truly, with a nonchalance we didn't feel, walked west on Prince Arthur to meet McC.

Near the corner of Durocher the managing editor appeared carrying a parcel which he handed to me with this soothing remark, "Here are the heaters—where is the car?"

The three of us then drove to a lane at the rear of Durocher Street where McCormick disappeared into one of the apartment houses. Within a few minutes, he returned with the much-sought-after Joe Miller.

Miller was wearing a colorful lumberjack shirt which could easily be spotted two miles down a coal mine. He was definitely not dressed to kill.

After saying hello all round he climbed into the rear of the car, calmly curled up on the floor and pulled a trench coat over himself. A husky six-footer, he showed no trace of nervousness. We noticed his hand was steady as he held a match to our cigarettes.

Therefore, with Miller on the floor in the rear of the car, Arless driving, yours truly sitting in the middle with a pair of guns balancing on two nervous knees, and McCormick sitting on our right discussing the merits of George Bernard Shaw, the ride to Verdun, which in our opinion makes Paul Revere's strictly a milk route, got off to a start.

We drove through the bright lights of Park Avenue without incident and turned west on Sherbrooke. Here the car light failed and, while all concerned held their breath, Arless tinkered with the wires for a few minutes before resuming the ride.

At Union Avenue, a traffic light broke all long distance records before turning green. A huge transport bus pulled up beside the sedan and passengers looked with dis-interest from the great height down on the car.

During this tense period, McCormick, still discussing Bernard Shaw's works, had decided "Pygmalion" was the writer's greatest effort: Miller asked from the rear floor our location, and yours truly did some plain and fancy praying. What Arless was thinking, Arless wasn't saying.

The remainder of the trip was uneventful and soon Miller was sitting nonchalantly sipping beer in the Verdun flat. He talked freely to McCormick, who took his story down while Miller posed readily for Arless' numerous photos.

During his stay at the Verdun address, countless friends, newsmen, etc., kept dropping in until the place looked something like Windsor station on a Labor Day weekend.

But if the residents of that tree-lined street wondered about the activity, they were too polite to investigate.

Miller remained there until the early hours of the morning, then he was transferred to *The Herald* building. Rumors that he was in the newspaper office soon spread around and staffers of a rival newspaper formed a picket line around the building.

Members of the police department who searched the building somehow overlooked the ladies' powder room, where Miller was reclining comfortably on a chaise longue. He later surrendered to Detective Bill Fitzpatrick and all concerned went home to get some much-needed sleep.

Following Miller's arrest, numerous subpoenas were

issued in the underworld. Also subpoenaed were several newspapermen. So great was the crowd in the witness room at Criminal Court that one subpoenaed gambler, more enterprising than his colleagues, produced a pack of cards a started a rip-snorting poker game.

Even before Miller was found guilty and sent up to serve a lengthy sentence the gambling gentry saw the handwriting on the wall; and it wasn't the results of the third at Hialeah. Public opinion flared up and the newspapers gave the underworld a hard time. Some major scale barbotte games moved to the rim of the town where they still operate just over the city limits.

Soon Montreal became as quiet as a rainy Sunday in Port Credit. A few of the lesser fry tried to sneak a fast game but the spirit—to say nothing of the action—just wasn't there.

A week previous to the Davis Slaying a homemade bomb was tossed at the rear window of a game operating at 1443 Mansfield Street. The pineapple fell short and exploded on the roof of Loew's Restaurant located below, tearing a two-foot hole in the ceiling, sprinkling plenty of plaster in the pastrami, but miraculously not harming anyone.

The underworld blamed Miller for the attack. Miller, a veteran of World War II, said nothing. If there was a link between the bombing and the Davis killing—no one ever forged it.

Although Miller was the most spectacular killer to give himself up to *The Herald*, he was by no means the last. Since his surrender it has become the thing to do.

Harold Gardner, young (26) city editor of the tabloid

has listened to several confessions ahead of the police department. So many, in fact that, at one time, he contemplated having a sign painted bearing the following message: "Confessions of Murder will be received between 9 a.m. and 5 p.m.—Weekdays only."

Characters, Characters—
Never Any Normal People

The old chestnut having to do with standing at the corner of 42nd Street and Broadway and eventually meeting every soul and heel you ever knew, does not apply to Montreal any more than it does to Manhattan.

But if you stand at the corner of Peel and St. Catherine (or St. Kit's as every native Montrealer calls it) chances are you'll be dunned for a sawbuck by either Jockey Fleming or Kid Ohblay. Once this has happened to you, you can boast to all and sundry that you are a recognized citizen enjoying the esteem of the community and a very definite part of Montrealia.

Fleming's territory extends westward from the corner of Peel Street on the south side of St. Kit's. His hated rival, Kid Ohblay, controls the corner diagonally opposite. Both are important characters in a town where characters abound.

Of the two, Fleming is slightly more colorful. His early history is rather fogged but it is generally believed that he is out of Newark, N.J. In the roaring twenties he was a singing waiter in an east end club and his rise to fame as one of the town's unofficial meeters and greeters has been meteoric—whatever that means.

So great is his importance that no sporting event can be considered even a minor success unless Fleming is present in the section usually reserved for millionaires, successful gamblers, visiting movie stars and used car dealers.

The Jock is much in demand at the numerous stag-parties thrown by the sporting gentry who need no excuse whatsoever to do so. At these rather dampish affairs, he is called upon at regular intervals to act as master of ceremonies or to sing. In fact no stag is complete unless Fleming renders a tear-jerking ballad in what is probably the world's worst baritone.

He reigns supreme as the Landlord of Peel Street and, apart from Kid Ohblay, no one yet has seriously disputed his claim. Visiting celebrities vie for the honor of inviting him to dinner. He knows—and this is important—and keeps more secrets of the underworld than any ten men.

Fleming's status as Montreal's One-Eyed Connolly was questioned on one occasion only—and that happened out of town. It seems the Jock decided to attend a ball game but was stopped at the gate by an unenlightened guard who, surprisingly, was not impressed by Fleming's title.

Our hero, bloodied but unbowed, enlisted the aid of a sympathetic barber who loaned him a white tonsorial jacket. Suitably clad in same, Fleming then collared a sympathetic store keeper who advanced him a supply of peanuts and a cardboard container. Armed thusly, Fleming walked through the gate with the battle cry of "Get them while they're hot" ringing through the stands.

Fleming's fame is by no means confined to Montreal. For instance, this writer was recently sitting with a friend in the bar of the Wofford Hotel in Miami Beach discussing (as all good Montrealers do) Montreal. The bartender, who had visited the town some 14 years previously, butted in on our conversation with, "How's Jockey Fleming?"

Not quite as famous, but equally as popular, Kid Ohblay, from his position across the intersection, is given to hurling insults at his rival from time to time. Every so often the feud goes into a lull and the pair retire to The Harmony Lunch for coffee and conversation. Anyone fortunate enough to be present at these armistices will be treated to more entertainment than can be had in the city where entertainment is a drug on the market.

It is not generally known that Ohblay holds honorable discharges from both wars. He is a native-born Montrealer and was a promising boxer more years ago than he cares to admit.

Like Fleming he is eagerly sought-after as a dinner companion. His small talk is studded with Montrealese jargon and his knowledge of Montreal is amazing. He is also a first rate tourist guide and is considered a good luck charm by a host of gambling friends.

The Kid probably outshone Fleming when the former was chosen for a role in the film "Montreal by Night," an ambitious undertaking by a local motion picture outfit. Some doubts were held along Peel Street as to the casting director's sanity when the Kid was given the part of an American tourist.

The scene showed Ohblay, suitably clad in the garb of someone's idea of a visiting Yankee, asking directions to Dominion Square. As all and sundry know, Kid Ohblay is familiar with evey pigeon around the Square and all agree that it took a brilliant effort on the part of our hero to play this role.

When the picture was premiered at an uptown theater, Ohblay took a position outside the place and signed autographs for an admiring throng. The crowd seemed to grow larger as the news spread around Peel Street that signatures were available. Noticeably absent from the throng—Jockey Fleming.

Following his success in "Montreal by Night" (his brief appearance was invariably greeted with thunderous applause) Ohblay toyed with the idea of joining the ranks of the thespians. We spent one hilarious evening in Slit-kin's with him during which the ex-lightweight champ Maxie Berger acted as elocution tutor.

The fact that Berger's vocabulary would be more at home around Madison Square Garden is not considered a major cause for Ohblay's decision to retire from the screen with but one triumph.

At the time of writing, both Ohblay and Fleming were around the corner and the town looked very normal as a result.

Among the more colorful personalities of yester-year, old-timers will recall playboy-sportsman Charlie Slabotsky. The Slab had a deep appreciation of fine food and a fast crap game. In the early Twenties he was a famil-iar figure around the St. Kit's and St. Lawrence Main area where his greatest achievements with the African dominoes were made.

In his heyday there was a dice game operating on St. Lawrence Main, just above Ontario which was patronized greatly by a pair of gamblers known as "The Boston Kid"

Club Lido on Stanley Street, 1931.
Joe Bell Scrapbook, Concordia University Archives, 2.p13a

STARTING
MONDAY

The One and Only

OSCAR
PETERSON

Starring Nightly in the

New Bamboo Lounge

Jerry Taylor's
TIC TOC

The Montreal Standard, October 8, 1949.
Meilan Lam fonds, Concordia University Archives, P135

and "Sporty George." Of the two, the Boston Kid created the greatest stir among Montrealers. He was from the wilds of Alberta and sported picturesque cowboy attire. He carried seemingly endless supplies of currency in a be-jeweled money belt. Sporty George, on the other hand, was a comparatively drab character. He wore somber dress and had a negative personality. His main claim to fame was his willingness to bet with anyone on anything at anytime.

One memorable night, the trio became engaged in a big-time crap game during which much heavy cabbage was gambled across the green baize. The Boston Kid, no one ever really knew why the Albertan was so-called, soon had the Goddess of Chance in his corner. Sporty George wasn't doing too badly either. But Slabotsky was enduring a major league run of bad luck.

Time came when The Slab got tapped out. He gazed about the room without spotting anyone capable of advancing him sufficient funds to continue the game, then walked out.

If you think a run of bad luck fazed the Slab, you don't know your old-timers. After leaving the game, he walked to the corner where Lesser's Clothing Store (now Gasco's) was featuring a sale of high-class suits.

Taking six suits from the rack on credit—and his credit was the best—he proceeded to peddle same among the playboys that abounded in the district. By selling the entire stock at $25 per, he realized $150 with which he returned to the game and cleaned it out.

Some old-timers who witnessed the play say the Slab took $50,000 from the game. Others claim it was closer to $100,000. Actually no one knew how much money was in action but it may be well to note that Slabotsky left Montreal shortly after and settled in Miami, where he now operates a liquor store.

Slabotsky was by no means the only colorful character around and about in those days. The same era produced the son of a wealthy industrialist who had a penchant for lengthy touring cars and long, cool drinks.

This character, young, handsome and wealthy, had a habit of getting beautifully stiff and driving his block-long car to a cafeteria on Peel Street near St. Kit's.

Each morning at dawning, the cafeteria manager was called upon to form a one-man jury to determine whether or not the gay young playboy was sober enough to enter for his morning coffee. Usually he wasn't in fit shape and was turned away with suitable apologies.

One morning, however, the playboy wanted a cup of coffee in the worst way and his refusal of admittance weighed heavily upon his mind. He appealed long and pitifully to the manager who remained polite but firm, thereby leaving him no choice but to return to his car, which was parked outside the door and contemplate a plan of attack.

After brooding for some half hour, he backed the car (a Lincoln) across Peel Street, shifting into second, stepped on the gas and aimed the car's ornate radiator cap at the plate glass window of the cafeteria. The force of the car against the flimsy make-up of the restaurant front resulted in both playboy and car gaining a noisy entrance into the eaterie. Miraculously, no one was hurt. For the record, it may be here noted that the playboy didn't get his cup of coffee and the damages were paid forthwith in great haste.

Another bon vivant who enlivened the same era had a habit of punching out both windows in a telephone booth before making a phone call. The same character would show up after a week's hunting trip, sporting a lengthy beard and two 12-gauge shotguns, at the Club Lido (the Tic Toc today) and insist that band leader Peter Barry (Pete's still around) play soft music until the early hours of the cold gray dawn.

The same character had a playful habit of tossing champagne bottles out of his hotel window. Full ones yet! This habit drove many hotel managers to an early grave. He would first barricade his door thereby making it necessary for police to chop up expensive hotel furnishings in order to gain admittance and halt the frothy blitz.

Another character—a rather obnoxious character, incidentally—was around in the early Thirties. His favorite haunt was the late, great Fabien Guérin's American Grill where Angelo Bisanti's American Spaghetti House is today.

This jerkeroo drank only double scotches and, before ordering the first drink, would obtain a box of matches. In those days book matches were not popular and for a penny one could get approximately 20 one-inch wooden ducifers.

Having obtained the aforementioned matches, the character would place them in his left-hand coat pocket and, upon ordering a drink, would transfer one match to his right-hand pocket. At the end of the evening he would ask for his tab but, before paying, would compare the number of matches in his right-hand pocket with the number of drinks for which he was charged.

As he was a stiff (waiter's parlance for a non-tipper), he was not the most welcome guest in the old American Grill. However, the character spent so much money the bosses insisted he be treated well.

One memorable night we were sitting at the next table to the obnoxious gent and watching with interest the slow burn endured by the waiter. We knew the lad would eventually be given a "Saratoga" (waiter's parlance for a padded rab) but we were wondering how it could be arranged.

The waiter (we won't mention his name but you know him well) gave us a knowing wink and asked the cigarette girl for three boxes of matches. These he emptied into his right hand and clutching a bill that looked like the national debt in his left hand, leaned over the troublesome customer.

We looked on, fascinated, as the waiter dropped the contents of three boxes of matches into the jerkeroo's pocket with his right hand while distracting him with the bill in his left. The character gazed through bleary eyes at the number of scorches he was being charged for and, much to the surprise of absolutely no one, complained that he was being taken.

"Oh no you don't," he mumbled, "I can prove exactly how many drinks I have had."

Whereupon he thrust his hand into his pocket and withdrew enough lumber to build a bridge. He paid and was not seen again around the American Grill.

Pax Means "Peace"

MONTREAL'S UNDERWORLD was still staggering under the blow it received by the murder of Harry Davis when an obscure police official, Pacifique Plante, delivered the knockout punch.

Plante—whom we nicknamed Pax—became boss-man of the Vice Squad during a period of confusion. Overnight he shed the cloak of a somewhat colorless lawyer and emerged as a rather delicate Daniel to face the lions.

He was given an office about the size of a healthy telephone booth, and was practically ignored by all concerned. Gamblers and other baddies did not consider him a threat to their business which they were desperately trying to rebuild. How wrong could they get!

Pax broke their collective hearts—if any. He was fanatically honest—a fact which they had overlooked and a virtue they couldn't comprehend. It is rumored that "Mr. District Attorney," as he was sometimes called, refused a flat offer of $200,000 in unmarked bills to lay off.

In any case, Pax went to work with a vengeance. Gambling joints were opened and closed with monotonous regularity. It soon became an expensive endurance contest, with Pax winning hands down.

Looking around for new vice to conquer Pax then went after the night clubs. For a time he would walk in unnoticed and sit unobtrusively in a corner sipping port wine. If any known hoods or prosties were present he

Pacifique "Pax" Plante (left) and Jean Drapeau assisted Justice François Caron in investigating organized crime and corruption in Montréal. Public outrage over the commission's findings swept Drapeau into power as the city's mayor.
John Gilmore fonds, Concordia University Archives, P004-02-295

would make a note of same and the nitery owner's life would be make miserable until the joint was either cleaned up or nominated for closure.

Cab drivers also fell under his watchful eye. He was the first to advocate placing pictures of all hackies within sight of the passenger. He weeded out known criminals—and others not so well known—from the ranks and, in general, created havoc with the business.

When he reported that he had been twice fired upon, gangsters volunteered to give the shooter a lesson—in target practice. It soon became evident that Pax was on his way out. And he was.

Then, just as suddenly as he had been forgotten, he was suddenly remembered. A series of articles appeared in the French Canadian daily newspaper *Le Devoir* signed by Pax and "exposing" conditions in the town. The claims were laden with dynamite—to make the understatement of the year. Soon a book appeared titled *Montréal sous le règne de la pègre* (Montreal Under the Reign of the Under-world), also by Pax, which just about clinched the deal.

The articles and book were greeted by an avalanche of libel suits and sparked a probe which will get underway just about the time this book gets on the newsstands.

Whether or not the fiery ex-lawyer can substantiate his claims remains to be seen. The usual, well-informed sources say he will seek a political career. Some hinted backing if he should run for mayor. If he does, the town will be treated to the greatest battle of words since Benjamin Franklin unsuccessfully tried to talk French Canadians into joining American forces during the war of independence.

Room—But Never Bored

MONTREAL'S FIRST HOTEL of note was Rasco's at 283 to 295 St. Paul Street near St. Claude. It was opened in 1836 by Romeo Rasco and was then the largest hotel in the city. It accommodated one hundred and fifty guests.

It was here that Mr. and Mrs. Charles Dickens signed the register when the author played the Theatre Royal. Other notables made the inn their headquarters during their stay here and the place set the style for future generations of hotel men.

Although there are several first-rate hotels in the city today there is still a severe shortage of accommodation for the thousands of tourists who flock here every week.

The Mount Royal is the largest and by far the most popular with the commercial trade. The Laurentien is favored by tourists and show people. The Ritz-Carlton gets the carriage trade and the Berkely the Social Register.

One of the best remembered inns among show people was the Ford, which for three decades livened up the corner of Bishop and Dorchester. The building has been taken over by the Canadian Broadcasting Corporation and will soon blossom forth as a pocket-sized radio city.

A few years back, the hotel was the headquarters show folks, wrestlers, newspapermen, musicians and other types of humans who make their living when the sun goes down to rest.

Life was anything but dull at the Ford. One wintery weekend, several hundred snowshoers descended on the place for a convention. No one seems to know what is discussed officially at a snowshoer's convention, but there is little doubt about what is consumed—during this one at least.

The snow lovers, clad in those corny outfits, ripped the furniture out of the lobby and held a rather alcoholic square dance. A battery of house detectives tried to break up the proceedings but were either ignored or themselves entangled in the twisting, turning screaming mob.

Strip-teaser Beverly King always lived there during her frequent local appearances. Shortly before show time one night the beauteous Beverly suddenly realized she couldn't remember where she had left her costume. Not the slightest bit dismayed, she took one of the drapes from the window and went through her act at the Versailles wearing that—and little else.

Before Murray's moved into the main floor space the room housed the Bishop Grill, an outsized combination bar and cabaret. Several attempts were made to introduce a floor show in the room but none was successful.

Almost every drinker has a floor show on New Year's Eve however, and the Bishop Grill was no exception. One year a complete chorus was included in the show, and thereby lies a tale, as someone said.

It seems the chorines met a few boys in Ligget's drug –store, which took up a fairly good-sized space in one corner of the lobby. Ligget's had a square lunch counter and the chorus gals and their newly-found loves were belting back stiff hookers as fast as was unwisely possible.

Came show time, and the gals, highly fortified with stagger syrup, wandered back to the Grill to do a number. The chorus made theatrical history that night and was considered a great success by those guests who could still see.

Without waiting to change into street clothes, the gals dashed back to Ligget's and their boyfriends. There ensued much more belting back of hookers and limited conversation. During the session, someone foolishly asked how the numbers went over.

This was a mistake. The gals, eager to show off their terpsichorean ability, climbed on the foot-wide counter and went through a rather stagger-laden recap of what had gone on in the Grill.

During its heyday, Ligget's remained open 24 hours a day and was the meeting place of what then passed for Café Society. The soda jerks who worked behind the fountain were treated as celebrities wherever they went. Among them were Mike Jerrow, Bill Peters, George Glezos, Nicky Kotsos and Andy Monette. Monette is now a waiter at the Jamaica Grill.

It was at Ligget's that Butch Buckler, the Manhattan producer, first met Jo-Jo Parker, whom he married. Jo-Jo, now known on Broadway as Josephine Boyer, was then in the chorus of the Casino de Paree.

With the closing of the Ford, a few dozen permanent guests were left homeless. Some moved to the Laurentien, others took apartments in the district and a few moved to other hotels. It was a sad move for all concerned.

More dignified, and much much quieter, the LaSalle Hotel on Drummond Street is a popular inn for show people. Lili St. Cyr stops here when she is in town and many other stellar attractions consider it their local home.

Originally a bachelor apartment building, the LaSalle has a distinctively French-Canadian atmosphere. Montrealers who know good food favor the Cavalier Café in the basement. Victor is the headwaiter and the place is a pleasant spot in which to dine.

Chorines favor the Esquire hotel on McGill College Avenue just north of St. Kit's. The Esky, as it is called, is a small, intimate place operated by one Peter Kotsonas who built it up from an obscure eating place known as the Ville de Paris to a super modernistic hotel.

Visitors unable to secure accommodation in a hotel are hereby warned to be careful what type of tourist room you rent for the night. Some are highly respectable establishments run by highly respectable inn-keepers—but there is also a great number of flea traps where you'll get little sleep and pay plenty for the privilege.

If you have baggage, several tourist homes will suddenly realize that they are filled to capacity. If this happens, you can pretty well take it for granted that you were expected to pay in advance and stay only an hour and then gettahell out let someone else hire the room. Well, what do you want us to do? Draw you a picture? It's an amateur bordello.

If you can't get into a hotel, your best bet is to ask the travel bureau in the lobby to recommend you a suitable tourist home.

There are several in the uptown area. Some are not worth the price asked, others are pleasant places in which to stay. If you can't find one, sleep in your car—many tourists do.

Slitkins and Slotkins,
Alive, Alive-O!

PROBABLY THE BEST KNOWN eat-and-drinkery is this ancient and honorable establishment over which Slitkin and Slotkin preside. Certainly no other restaurant has been so widely publicized and no other restaurateurs have been privileged to read as much data on their comings and goings as have Messrs. S & S.

The jaw-breaking handle of Slitkins and Slotkins was tagged on the two dealers in new and used prize fighters who were christened Lou Wyman and Jack Rogers. The nickname was taken from a comedy act which played the Gayety Theatre many years ago.

The Pair have been partners for some quarter century and had many downs before enjoying the current series of ups. They are direct opposites in personality and appearance. Wyman is short, slender and soft-spoken. Rogers is tall, portly and gregarious. One thing they have in common, however, is a shrewd knowledge of the prize-fighting game.

They got into the restaurant business as a natural climax to a sometime successful period of promoting pugilists. Their first bistro proved they could draw a steady stream of customers who were fascinated by their ability to serve good food and mangle the King's English.

During the war, they bought out a spaghetti parlor

on Dorchester Street near Mountain and opened what was destined to be one of the most colorful restaurants in the city.

Rogers acts as front man while Wyman stands guard over the cash register. The combination has been a successful one, as any customer will note by the number of autographed pictures on the wall.

On fight nights, it is difficult to find a table in the place and, with prizefighters at every table, it is unwise to tell anyone to push over and make room.

The upstairs lounge is known as the "Chez When Room" and features caricatures of newspapermen and various celebrities. Also upstairs is the Irish Room, where banquets, stags and other get-togethers are held almost nightly.

Before the Montreal Press Club opened, "Slit's" served in that capacity. Today, although not so plentiful, you'll find at least one scribe in the place at any given hour. You'll also see Lili St. Cyr—a regular customer when she's in town—and practically every sportsman ever to visit Montreal.

Where They're At

IF RADIO PERSONALITIES interest you and you've always wanted to see what that swoon-voiced announcer looks like, try Dinty Moore's on St. Kit's, opposite the King's Hall Building. Most radio announcers, as well as musicians, technicians, actors and producers, can be found between shows in the Ship Ahoy room at those tables close to the bar (wise pipple!)

Advertising types and dance studio instructors eat at Drakes at the southwest corner of Stanley and St. Kit's. You'll find the cuties (who can teach you your left foot from your right faster than your sergeant-major did) sitting close to the window, sipping malteds and resting their tootsies between lessons.

Show people invariably wind up at the Chic-N-Coop after their clubs have closed. You'll see chorus girls wearing full make-up, plus musicians, performers and the occasional niterie boss chewing spare ribs with gusto each and every morning just before dawn. The Coop is also a favorite eating and meeting place for baseball players, wrestlers and other members of the musical gentry.

Waiters, hackies, busboys and such usually breakfast at the Laurentian Restaurant on Dorchester Street near Slitkins. This spot is also popular with acts from Rockhead's and the St. Michel. "Smokey," the senior salami slicer, who presides regally over the pastrami, can tell you

Montreal singer Norma Hutton with Frank Sinatra
at the Chic-N-Coop, February, 1953.
Alan Hustak fonds, Concordia University Archives, P191-02-01

more history about the town's night life than any one of his tender years has a right to know.

Models, photographic and otherwise, can be found any afternoon in Macy's at the northeast corner of Stanley and St. Kit's or one block further east in Brysons' Drug Store. You can't tell them by the hatbox they carry because they don't carry hatboxes.

Executive types and members of the city's blue bloods frequent Café Martin or Drury's. Café Martin serves the finest French food this side of the Eiffel Tower, while Drury's is an English-type chop house with a menu that will set any true-blue Britisher to looking up ships sailing to Blighty. The atmosphere at both places is quiet and dignified and if you are going to close any business deals, either one of these places is highly recommended as the scene of the dotted-line-signing and such.

The Younger Degeneration

UNLIKE TORONTO and other western cities Montreal is not plagued by zoot suiters. During the war, a few juve delinks sported the ridiculous drapes unmolested. Time came, however, when a few youths wearing zoots made the inexcusable mistake of beating up a seaman.

In no time whatsoever the uptown streets were jam-packed with irate sailors from both the navy and the Merchant Marine, all ready, willing and able to take the zooters apart. When one was found, he was stripped and given a workout by the tars and sent home. Some zooters were seriously injured by the goings-over handed out and, since then, for some reason or other, zoot suiters are rarely seen.

Like all big cities, Montreal has a juvenile delinquent problem. But it is no more serious than that of any other city of its size and far less serious than many smaller cities.

Apart from the Griffintown gangs of yesteryear, no organized gang of hoodlums created sufficient trouble to remain remembered very long. The Bordon gang, which terrorized the North End 25 years ago, and which made a specialty of breaking the legs of anyone so unfortunate as to incur their displeasure, lasted but a short time before being dissolved.

A few groups of teen-aged hoodlums hung out behind the old Delorimier Race Track and fought it out with BB guns and sling shots every so often. They did not, however, come close to attaining the doubtful fame of Toronto's Beanery Gang—or maybe they just didn't have as good a press agent.

The Fabulous El

WITH THE POSSIBLE EXCEPTION of the Frolics, no other night club will be remembered as long, nor as fondly, as will El Morocco, which stood at the northwest corner of Metcalfe and St. Kit's.

Originally opened by Arthur Davidson, who had planned a gambling layout on the top floor, the spot passed to a group of sportsmen who operated it until the Spring of 1949 when the lease ran out and the building came down to make way for the bank which now occupies the site.

Two of the owners, Yvon Robert the wrestling idol of French Canada, and Eddie Quinn, the promoter, attracted visiting celebrities in such numbers that the place became famous throughout Canada and the United States.

Anyone who was anyone visited the El. It was not unusual to see Jack Dempsey, Max Waxman and Jack Sharkey discussing the fight business in one corner while, at another, a group of clergymen were quietly discussing whatever clergymen discuss over dinner.

The club raised fantastic sums of money for charity. It was standard routine to take the entire band, show and chorus to veterans' hospitals for performances and no worthwhile organization was ever refused aid by the four partners.

Comedian Willie Shore, 1947, played at the El Morocco, corner
of Metcalfe and St. Catherine streets.
Photo: Bruno of Hollywood.
Al Palmer Fonds, Concordia University Archives, P084-02-80,

The El had the prettiest chorus girls, the funniest comics, the thickest steaks and the strongest drinks. Shows were ambitious ventures and featured such top ranking comics as Willie Shore, Buddy Lester, Paul Grey, Jack E. Leonard, Jackie Miles, Doc Marcus, Jerry Bergen, Alan Gale, etc.

The staff was considered the finest tray-trotting talent ever to be assembled in one night club at one time. Former NHL hockey star Jimmie Orlando was manager. René Campeau, now at the Bellevue Casino, was head-waiter.

Others included waiters Rudy, now at the Indian Room, Bob, now headwaiter at the Folies Bergéres, Eddie, now bartender at the same spot, Roland, now bartender at Aldo's, Al MacDonald and Gino Lombardo, both of whom are presently in Toronto. There were several others who helped make the club great, but they are too numerous to list here.

The last days of the El were the dampest on record. On its final night, a rather sad farewell party was held with champagne flowing like the St. Lawrence. The party grew damper and sadder as dawn went into bat for dusk. At nine o'clock in the morning, while demolition crews were at work tearing down the building, the celebrants were still celebrating, sadly and damply.

Rocky Goldberg, who handled the backstage bar, and Hickey, who operated the spotlight for the shows, refused to leave the place until convinced a new El would soon re-open on a different site.

Although it operated for the brief span of five years, it has yet to be replaced as the spot where "everybody goes." If you get too nostalgic reading these lines ,drop in to The Continental at St. Urbain and St. Kit's. The beloved mahogany bar, upon which leaned all and sundry, is now in operation there.

"The El had the prettiest chorus girls, the funniest comics."
Al Palmer fonds, Concordia University Archives, scrapbook, July 23, 1955.

Casino De Whoopee

EVEN AS EL MOROCCO was gasping its last gasps and night clubbers were looking around for a new place to live, Harry "Don't Say I'm Smart" Holmok opened the largest night club in the Dominion, The Bellevue Casino.

Holmok, who comes as close to being a Canadian Ziegfeld as anyone, will long be remembered as the night club man who lost three liquor licenses in the space of a year. It was Holmok who shoe-stringed a hamburger stand on the east side into the highly successful Vienna Grill, then parlayed it into the Bellevue.

Although operating one successful nitery after another, he ran into more tough breaks than enough. Before opening the Bellevue, he studied the situation for nine years. During this period he convinced himself that he knew what the taxpayers wanted.

His first step was to buy the Roseland Dancehall on Ontario Street, just west of Bleury. This done, he installed a mammoth stage and, amid sad shaking of heads on the part of the town's alleged wise guys, told all concerned that he was going to open a night club. One of his partners promptly walked out.

Everyone along Nightclub Alley thought Holmock had gone soft in the head—including this writer. The place was too big, spenders wouldn't go that far east, Holmok would go broke and other encouraging remarks were bandied about while he was getting the place into shape.

No one was more right than Holmok. On opening night the crowd lined up for two blocks or so. The carriage trade and the east end mob jammed the velvet rope trying to get a table—any table—and waiters worked to exhaustion attempting the impossible task of keeping the crowd supplied.

From opening night on, the place has been jammed, but Holmok still refuses to admit that he was smart. "Anyone who gives the public what it wants just can't miss," is his usual reply to any flattering remarks.

The shows are extravagant productions with the accent on girls and novelty acts. No act takes more than a solitary bow, hence the presentations never lag. So far, acrobats, jugglers, animal acts, etc., have played the spot and there is little doubt but that Holmok would book in an elephant act if he thought the public would like it.

Although the Bellevue is too big a club to hold the intimate atmosphere of El Morocco, you'll see most of the former El habitués there. Also there is the team of Goldberg and Hickey and many of the chorines who trod the light fantastic at the El.

The Play's the Thing

MONTREAL'S SHOW BUSINESS history dates back to 1774, when a group of British GI's went into a huddle and came up with a few plays which they held in small unheated rooms. As accommodation was limited, actors frequently were called upon to emote while their teeth chattered. The efforts of the soldiers nevertheless gained a foothold in the city during an era when play-acting was considered only slightly more respectable a profession than stealing horses.

First big time showplace to get into action was the Theatre Royal which opened on St. Paul Street in 1825. It was reported to have cost in the neighborhood of $40,000 which, in those days of penny beers, was a very expensive neighborhood indeed.

The immortal Charles Dickens made his debut as an actor at Theatre Royal, which automatically placed the house on the theatrical map. It soon became the gathering place of society with the carriage trade keeping the turnstiles clicking. No popcorn was sold.

Another Theatre Royal was built on Coté Street in 1852. This, too, was a huge success, with the greatest theatre names of England and Europe listed on its playbills. One prominent thespian of that time, Edmund Kean, played there and his performance was attended by a great number of Indians. Kean was immediately made an honorary chief and left with a very good impression of Montreal and a chieftain's be-feathered headdress.

The play definitely is still the thing in Montreal. There is an active and ambitious Repertory theatre, a group who present Shakespeare in the fresh air of the mountain, various church drama clubs, etc.

Vaudeville, the wayward offspring of the music hall, reached the peak of its popularity at the Imperial Theatre on Bleury Street a few decades back. Almost every headliner up to and including Weber and Fields trod its boards and there was much wailing and weeping when the house charged its policy to motion picture presentation.

Loew's picked up where the Imperial left off and ran as a three-a-day house for several years. Arthur Schalek, vaudeville's official historian locally, reveals that Loew's was an important date on the circuit and attracted the cream of the theatrical crop, including many movie biggies.

Stiff competition from night club floor shows is credited with turning theater vaudeville into a lost cause. Some smaller theaters make an earnest effort now and then to revive it but usually bow out after a few dismal days of box office famine.

Today there is one big time vaude house in operation—the Gayety, managed by showman Tommy Conway. If you are going to call this burlesque, don't come right out and say so in front of Conway, or he'll drag you into a corner and prove to you that you're wrong—in a few well frozen words.

The Gayety is sometimes called "The House That Lili Built" and if you're curious to know why, try to buy a ticket when the marquee bills Lili St. Cyr. It's like trying to get a ducat to South Pacific.

Miss St. Cyr—her name is actually Marie Van Schaak—is a tall, shapely, platinum-tressed Californian who spreads an epidemic of striptacoccus here several times per year when she appears.

It is not considered an unusual occurrence if traffic is blocked by eager patrons of the arts milling around the box office trying to buy tickets when Lili is appearing. The gambling gentry will lay you terrific odds that she will outdraw any attraction that plays the city.

There has been much talk about placing a life-sized statue of her in the lobby of the theater. Many Montrealers have advanced the idea of having the statue placed in a prominent square. Whether the statue is placed in the theater or in a park is open for debate.

The fact remains, however, that she is the all-time favorite of the show-going population. No other act has enjoyed such repeated success, and no other stripper has been as highly paid.

Burlesque made its bare-faced debut in Montreal at—of all places—the Theatre Royal on Coté and Craig [now Viger] where the Montreal Tramways terminal stands today. It operated in 1908 and among those who appeared there was heavyweight champ Jack Johnson. Part of Johnson's chores on the stage included the exhibiting of what he claimed to be the world's thinnest watch. It was about the thickness of a fifty-cent piece.

No one seems to recall the names of the strippers who graced the Royal but, strangely enough, everyone around at that time remembers that the theater was raided when one doll's version of a hoochy-coochy brought down the house—also the law.

There are still a few bush-league burlesque houses operating on Lower Main Street but The Gayety—where big time vaudeville reigns supreme—gets the heaviest play.

Lili St. Cyr: "No other stripper has been as highly paid."
Po84-02-322, Al Palmer fonds (Po84).
Photo: John E. Reed, Hollywood.

African Acres

MONTREAL'S HARLEM runs west from Windsor Street on St. Antoine to just beyond Mountain. It is a dismal area with rickety houses, run down shops, all of which are covered by a layer of dense smoke from the nearby railway lines.

At one time, it was a rough, tough district with knifings, shootings, muggings and other such off-shoots of dire poverty, occurring nightly. There were more speakeasies to the block in the district than any other section of the city.

Strangely enough, Whites caused most of the trouble in the area. They opened blind pigs with little more than a bottle opener and a prayer and attracted the worst elements of the city to the St. Antoine Street district.

One lusty, blustery spot was operated by a genial gent known only as Boston Joe. Boston was a likeable character and a very fast man with a buck. However, he had little opportunity of keeping undesirable types out of his spot and for a few years was a thorn in the side of the police department.

Another wild and wooly speak was operated for two years as a one-night per weeker. It opened at one o'clock every Wednesday morning and was a favorite haunt of musicians who would squeeze into the spot and jam around until noon.

There was no color line then, any more than there is today, and the fights were fierce and frequent. One particularly interesting feature of the joint was that the music never stopped during the brawls. How it operated unmolested for such a length of time is one of Ourtown's minor mysteries.

Wedged between the brothels, barbotte games and blind pigs were a handful of licensed night clubs. The Beacon, located just west of Windsor on St. Antoine, ran for a few years with a Negro song and dance man known as "Stringbeans" Price acting as perennial master of ceremonies. The show usually consisted of third rate White acts.

More famous than the Beacon—more expensive, too—was the Terminal Club ,which was located on St. Antoine in the building now occupied by the rooming house which advertises (in neon lights, yet) "Running Water."

The Terminal drew the social and the cash registers and was noted for its torrid entertainment. The house specialty was a potent rum drink known as a "Tobago Teaser," the brainchild of senior mixologist Wilfy Crooks. The concoction was fully guaranteed to spread your toes at each gulp.

Today there are only two cabarets in the district: Rockhead's Paradise (rapidly becoming an institution) on the southeast corner of St. Antoine and Mountain, and Café St. Michel whose flashy exterior can be found on Mountain Street almost directly opposite.

Rockhead's is operated by Rufus Rockhead, the unofficial mayor of the Negro colony. He is a soft-spoken, impeccable and deeply religious man whose daughter

(Top) Dancers at the Terminal Club take a break.
(Bottom) Terminal Club M.C. and singer, Babe Wallace.
Concordia University Archives

Mae Johnson Stars At Terminal Club

Replacing Babe Wallace, who has joined Ella Fitzgerald's orchestra in capacity as Maestro, is the swingsational cotton club star Mae Johnson, whose magnetic personality and outstanding talent has been the talk of the Great White Way in New York. No less a versatile entertainer is Mae Diggs making her initial appearance in Montreal.

Then there is the exotic Lucille O'Daniel rendering her conception of an Oriental fantasy and Sara Cheek gives out with a novelty song "You, You, You." Bubbles and Millie swing out a terrifc dance routine and Ed. Perkins dispenses dance-inducing music. Grace Allen rounds out the floor-show in steliar fashion.

Terminal Club publicity, 1940.
Montreal Standard, Meilan Lam fonds,
Concordia University Archives, P135

attended McGill University. The St. Michel, at one time, changed its owners almost as regularly as it changed its floor shows. At time of writing, it is owned by a French Canadian.

There is little difference between the shows at these two clubs. Both are noisy, sexy and have plenty of bounce. St. Michel offers better music which is played by Louis Metcalf and his International Orchestra.

Strangely enough, the first colored show to play Montreal was not presented in a colored night club. It was booked into the Cosy Grill on St. Catherine Street, opposite Eaton's.

At that time, the Cosy was operated by the Demetre Brothers, George, Tony and Mike—all youngsters. Among top rate Negro talent to play there was the famous Babe Wallace.

It was George Demetre who originated the cigarette girl idea. During a period when White shows were playing the Cosy, a young girl named Pearl Fields was singing sweet music with the show. A great kidder, George Demetre complained to her that the bar wasn't selling enough cigarettes to pay for the bother it was to keep them.

Pearl, no second-rate gangster herself, joked that she could sell them faster than the bar. Taking a stock, she emptied them into a cardboard carton and walked around the club. At the end of the week, she found she had earned $90. Her singing career was promptly abandoned. She is now at Aldo's Café—still selling cigarettes.

The Cosy's success with colored revues led to a wave of similar shows throughout the city. At one time the Chinese Paradise startled night club goers by presenting Negro revues and hiring a Negro band.

Although both Rockhead's and the St. Michel are Negro clubs, the customers are predominantly White. Unlike New York's Harlem, Whites are rarely molested in the local Negro district.

Most Black Belt inhabitants live quiet industrious lives. Few remain long in the area, preferring rather, to live in the northern section of the city or in Verdun.

The district has produced several brilliant doctors, lawyers and musicians. Of the latter, Oscar Peterson, the child prodigy of the piano, is best known. Peterson stood New York on their collective ear during a stay at Manhattan's Bop City.

Father Devine has a well-attended Heaven located in the district and his followers congregate regularly to sing his praises. On the western outskirts of the district is a shoe shine parlor operated by one of his "Angels." There is nothing unusual in the general appearance of the shop that would distinguish it from any of the other tired-looking establishments that line the street, except for a profusion of signs with such startling messages that there is no charge for shoe shines and, "Thank you, Father."

The place is operated by a cheerful (and disgustingly healthy) Negro who doesn't ask for payment for his services. Any donation—or none at all—is greeted with "Thank You, Father." This writer interviewed him one day and must honestly confess that we found him to be the most contented man we have ever met.

Favorite eating place of the district is owned by a dour Negro who came up from the United States to operate a barbeque restaurant on St. Antoine, opposite *The Gazette* building.

Specialty here is barbequed spare ribs seasoned with the finest sauce you're likely to find on this or any other continent. The recipe of the sauce is jealously guarded and much sought after. One night a group of students poured some of it in a bottle and announced solemnly that they intended bringing it to the lab at McGill and analyzing it. This almost created a race riot.

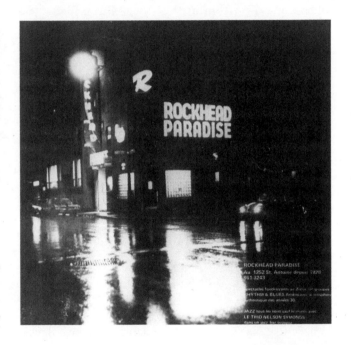

Rockhead's Paradise shortly before it closed in 1977, the missing apostrophe the result of Quebec's 1974 language law. *P078-02-01. Concordia University Archives Jazz collection (P078)*

Caprice Chinois

THE SPARKLE THAT WAS CHINATOWN'S has lost most of its luster since the disastrous fire in the Winter of 49-50 when a good portion of the area went up in flames, claiming the lives of more than a dozen people.

The district extends westward on Lagauchetière Street from St. Lawrence Main and takes in a mere two blocks. You'll note a few pagodas here and there but they are strictly for the benefit of tourists and the people who manufacture neon tubing.

The last night club to operate there was the Chinese Paradise, situated on the north side of the Street near Clark. It ran for several years and was the place to visit inasmuch as the food was good, although the floor shows were only fair.

One summer evening shortly before the war, a fierce fight broke out in the place. No one ever really knew what started it, but in no time whatsoever it graduated into a combination Donnybrook and Pier Sixer.

The battle raged for approximately two hours during which customers tore the legs from tables and conked their fellow customers over the head with same. It was a lulu. Petite Lola Milroy who was dancing on the bill ,was herded from the place by a cab driver who fought his way through the melee.

Details of the scrap echoed through the court rooms for some time, but too many persons were involved to

Advertisement for the Chinese Paradise.
(Date and source unknown.)
Myron Sutton Scrapbook, Concordia University Archives,
S.1p36e

actually clear the air and find the cause. The Paradise re-opened but was never quite the same again.

There is no floor show to be seen in Chinatown today, unless we count the antics of taxpayers trying to feed their faces with chop sticks and managing only to keep the dry cleaners in business.

Time was when the RCMP had their immigration cells in a basement on the north side of the Street. The fact that it was a basement hoosegow led many naïve souls to perform weird mental calisthenics and come up with the white-slavery-dope-den idea.

Local Chinese keep mostly to themselves. In pre-war days many enterprising ones ran Chinese lotteries as wide open as it was possible to be. Now, however, gambling is confined among themselves and it is a rare event indeed when a game is raided.

There are few Japanese in the city. McGill lists a handful among its students and Arthur Murray's studio had one on its teaching staff—a real looker—and there are probably a few others around town—but not many. The 1941 census revealed their number to be a mere 41.

A few years ago, a group came from British Columbia and attempted to make Montreal conscious of Japanese cooking. They opened a suki-yaki place over the Maroon Club (where St. Moritz Roof is now) and went through the whole deal of cooking vegetables right at your table.

The food was good but not sensational, and although the place was decorated in a lavish manner, customers stayed away in great numbers and finally the attempt was considered a failure. Peter Barry's band was booked into the room and it soon flourished as a rumba house.

Revelry by Night

ASK ANY TEN OLDTIMERS the name and location of Montreal's first night club and it's a lead pipe cinch that you'll get ten different answers.

Lumpkin's, on the northwest rim of the town, operated during the turn of the century but was not a night club. In 1912 there was a roadhouse known as Dupere's, down east near the former site of Dominion Park. It was owned by an alderman.

This writer, a minor-league old timer, hereby risks ridicule, scoffs, like "yah don't know what ya talkin' about," invitations to fight it out behind the club, and the wrath of everyone over 50 years of age by claiming the first night club to operate—that is, night clubs as we know them today—was The Parisian, which stood on the north-east corner of St. Dominique and St. Kit's, where the Broadway Hotel is today. And we have Sammy Vineberg to back up the argument.

The Parisian featured a floor show and was known as a cabaret. Although the word "cabaret" is a New Orleans expression used to denote a combination coffee house, saloon, brothel and gambling dive, the Parisian featured only good drinks and a show.

It was opened during World War One by a chap by the name of Gravel and burned down soon after. Gravel later opened a spot called the Regal Café Rathskeller in The Jacobs Building on St. Catherine, just east of Phillip's Square.

In 1918 the place became known as The St. Regis Cabaret and could accommodate 600 persons. The decorations were the most lavish Montrealers had seen up to that time. A branch of The Northeastern Lunch now occupies the site, and if you look closely you'll still see the decorations your Pop raved about 'way back when.

In 1919 Billy Cohen opened a spot on the east side of Bleury Street, just above St. Kit's. It was originally named The Blue Bird and later The Claridge. The spot was a plushy rendezvous for the monied citizenry of that day.

During the early 20s, Puss Milaire opened a roadhouse that was to become one of the best-remembered in night club history. It was located on St. Lawrence Boulevard north of Cremazie and bore the improbable name of The Motorists' Inn. It featured, among the pleasantries, a gambling room upstairs.

Sailor Sigmand and George Dussault bought the place from Milaire and operated it successfully for a short period, then sold out to a trio of highly experienced café men: Phil Maurice, Billy Cohen and Sam Vineberg.

With so much night club talent running the place, it couldn't miss. However, the trio split up a few years later with Maurice leaving to operate a long string of high-class cabarets. His first was called the Old Heidelberg and was located at the corner of St. Alexander and Mayor.

Billy Cohen was out of action for awhile but soon got back into business with the New Yorker, which occupied the space in which the bar of The Carousel is now located. Sammy Vineberg became a waiter at The Frolics.

Today Phil Maurice (who gave the name to Chez Maurice, incidentally) is in the theater business. Billy

Cohen has retired and Sammy Vineberg is with a distillery.

There were several other elaborate spas operating at the same time. One, the Brass Rail on Drummond Street, featured a solid glass dance floor. The Pagoda, The Venetian Gardens and The Dreamland Café were other well-remembered night haunts.

The Dreamland was located on the southwest corner of Ontario and St. Lawrence and made the headlines when a musician was shot dead in the place. The shooting wasn't part of the floor show. There are several different versions of what actually happened.

Eye witnesses who were there that night deny there was any tie-up in a gangland slaying, as was believed by many. What actually happened goes like this: A hold-up man wearing two particularly business-like guns, entered and ordered everyone to kick in with their valuables. An American tourist, sitting near the entrance playfully threw a chair at him.

Meanwhile a drummer from the Belmont Park orchestra decided to make a dash for cover behind the service bar. As the chair hit the gunsel, the gunsel fired and hit the drummer just like that.

The Jardin de Danse is best remembered for its famous band—The Melody Kings, which was made up of such greats as Andy and Johnny Tipaldi, Billy Munro, Bob Williams, Harry Luce and other talented music makers.

Billy Munro, who claims authorship of the tune "When My Baby Smiles at Me," is still playing around the town. He drives a Buick convertible of fire-engine red which is easily recognized. His son Billy Junior is an athlete of note. Harry Luce is now playing bass with Russ Meredith's Dixieland combo at the Little Bellevue Café.

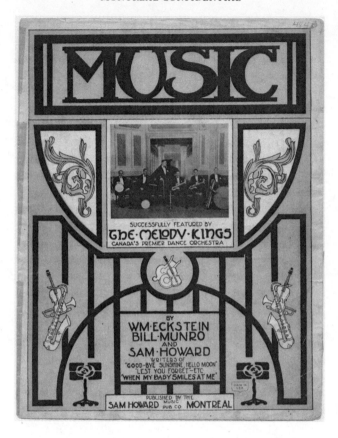

"Music (Makes the World Go 'Round,)" sheet music (1923)
with an image of the Melody Kings in Montreal.
*Sam Howard Music Pub. Co., Alex Robertson Collection,
Concordia University Archives, P023-S-0484*

The Hardened Artery

WHETHER YOU'RE LOOKING for a gal or a gun, a haircut or a hustler, a hock shop or a hamburger—you'll find it on St. Lawrence Boulevard.

This ribbon of concrete stretches north to south through the center of the city. It is a ribbon which Montreal wears not too proudly in her hair.

Sometimes it is called "The Oriental Main." No one seems to know where the tag "Oriental" comes in but it is easy to see why the term "Main" applies. The city's numbering system east and west springs from the street.

North of Ontario, the Main becomes the Jewish district. There are approximately 70,000 Jews in the city and their businesses are either located on The Main or had their origin on the street.

Going north from Ontario Street, it is a jumble of rickety dwellings leaning, in some case, wearily against modern structures for support. The further north you go, the tamer—and cleaner—the street becomes.

But below Ontario—brother-r-r.

At the St. Kit's angle you'll find the riff raff of the world scurrying around like wharf rats. Here you'll probably be offered—for a reasonable price—the watch that was stolen from you as you crossed the opposite corner.

The section between Craig Street and St. Kit's is the

nearest approach to an old-fashioned, knock-'em-down and drag-'em-out Tenderloin as you're apt to see in Canada. It is rough, tough, lusty and lewd. If you're looking for trouble, here is where you'll find it. And don't say we didn't warn you.

This section is the favorite stamping grounds of visiting sailors. There are tattooing parlors, Skid Row beaneries and you can get a haircut for a few cents—providing you're not too particular. If you're particular at all, you can go to the barber college and let a student go to work on your head. Who knows?—maybe you'll get one who is just about to graduate.

There are plenty of cheap movie houses where the pictures shown are not too noisy and you may get a bit of sleep. There is also an abundance of flop houses where you can rest your weary head for two bits. If your fellow guests lead you to think you have walked into an audition for the Snake Pit—what do you expect for two bits?

It is not unusual for Montreal's Upper Strata to organize an evening in the district for the simple purpose of mingling with the shady characters and getting huge gobs, but gobs, my deah, of atmosphere from the area.

Despite the shoddy surroundings, there are several first-rate night clubs in the section. The plushy Folies Bergères is located just south of St. Kit's and serves Blue Bloods and tourists in great numbers.

The Folies was formerly called the El Patio, a barn-sized niterie with a French-Canadian's idea of what Mexican atmosphere is like. The place staggered along at a fair clip until converted into a swankey night club. There is a balcony running around the spot, which seems to be the gathering place of celebrities.

The shows are good and the chorus is made up of El Morocco graduates and other pretties from New York booking offices. The staff, headed by headwaiter Robert, or Bob, is one of the most efficient in the town. All in all, it will give you the impression of being a pocket-sized Bellevue Casino with a more intimate atmosphere.

On the opposite side of the street and a bit further north, is Au Faisan Doré (the Golden Pheasant) which occupies a spot that has been a night club for some thirty years. This writer has visited the place when it was known under the tags of The Frolics, Connie's Inn, The Casino de Paree, The Val d'Or and the present name.

The place was once a theater. It graduated from a factory. Was a store house. A garment business was carried on for some time, as well as a few other industries, then it became a night club.

The most famous club to occupy the spot was The Frolics, which flourished there in the early Thirties. Texas Guinan and her girls opened the place amid much celebration on the part of all concerned.

An entire book could be written about The Frolics. It was the most ambitious night club venture ever to be undertaken in the town up to that time.

Among the owners who sliced up the take from the fabulous oasis were the Hill Brothers, Eli, Lou, Cece and Vic. The Hill boys were considered the smartest brother team in local night club business at that time and are still considered so today. They opened the Chic-N-Coop just before the war and turned the place into the Montreal equivalent of Manhattan's Lindy's. As an encore to that success, they added a fantastically beautiful drinking spot as an annex and called it the Indian Room.

Another Frolics partner was Charley (The Chauffeur) Bordoff who now operates the Drummond Café on the Street of the same name. Bordoff is a quiet gent with a wry sense of humor.

One night a group of four yokels came into the club each carrying a bulky parcel. Mac MacDonald, the headwaiter at that time, gave them a ringside table more or less as a gag on Sammy Vineberg, the waiter on duty at the station.

Vineberg looked the party over critically and immediately informed them that there was a five-bucks-a-head cover charge. They all smiled. He asked for their order and they smiled again saying they didn't want anything but they'd gladly pay the cover charge. Whereupon they opened the parcels and withdrew several quart bottles of beer.

It was bad enough that the club only served pints of beer and very few of those—but the fact that the customers were bringing their own supply proved too much for Vineberg.

He made a mad dash to the rear of the club where the partners sat looking on the scene with amusement. "What will I do?" cried Sammy. "Look. They brought their own bottles, yet!"

The partners remained silent for a moment, then Bordoff turned to Vineberg and uttered this classic: "Bring them some glasses. Do you want our customers should have to drink out of bottles?

The spot soon became a show place. The walls were

paneled with silk and the chairs and tables cost a small fortune. One night after the club had operated successfully for a few years, a weary customer leaned back to stretch his arms. Unfortunately he had a lighted cigar in his hand which touched the silken walls, and in no time whatsoever The Frolics became a memory.

Texas Guinan played there twice and her familiar greeting, "Hello Sucker," was acknowledged by most of the wealthy stay-out-all-nighters of that period.

On her second engagement, a young up-and-coming comic played on the same bill. He was unknown at the time and all and sundry wondered what a kid of that age was doing in a night club. There was nothing youngish about his act, however, and he soon became one of America's funny men. We mean Alan Gale.

Gale broke a record of some kind or other during his engagement there. It seems he was living at a nearby hotel which, at that time, was having trouble with its heating system.

One frosty morning, Gale returned to his room to find it as cold as an army conscription notice. He was carrying a forty-ounce bottle of Canadian Club which should have cheered him up no end. However, although there was hot water in the taps, there was none in the radiator and, despite the formidable heating equipment he was carrying, he still felt cold.

After a frigid debate with himself, he emptied the forty-ouncer down the sink and filled the bottle with hot water from the tap. Using this as a foot warmer he crawled into bed. There are several characters around the town that still hold a grudge against him for this sort of behavior.

Gale returned to play Montreal almost yearly before giving up traveling. At present he is a near neighbor of ours and owns the plushy Celebrity Club on 22nd Street in Miami Beach.

In the Middle Thirties, Nick Materas opened the place under the name of Casino de Paree. It was a flossy, glossy spot but had no silken walls. It operated under various owners and various managers for some time before being changed to the Val d'Or.

Sammy Lipson managed the spot during its salad years. He had a mania for surprising his customers by going to extremes with his shows. For instance, one week he featured The Beef Trust Revue, a dainty group of dolls who weighed in the neighborhood of 350 pounds apiece. Star was Tiny Sinclair who did a take off on a strip teaser but who appeared wearing red flannel underwear and using papier mâché sewer covers instead of fans.

The following week, Lipson, in one of his rare moments, booked in a complete midget show. The tiny folks were such a contrast to the gigantic Amazons, people began to talk and there was much speculation as to what Lipson would book in next. The showman, he is now with Bond's in Toronto, once told yours truly that he was looking for a pair of two-headed tenors so that they could sing the quartet from "Rigoletto" in half the usual time.

Another colorful gent who brain-trusted the spot was Dave Bernie. Known as a fashion plate around the town, he returned from New York after a not-too-successful career as a song and dance man. As a manager who knew practically everybody worth knowing in town, he found himself in the right spot. He could emcee his own shows—which he often did—and could fill in with a song or dance or some witty patter, which he also did. He also had a rare gift for getting free publicity for the club. Bernie now operates the Forum Delicatessen and has retired permanently from the night club business.

Today the club is the haunt of those looking for that Montmartre atmosphere. Shows are strictly French and there is an outsized dance floor with a fairly good band to keep it reasonably crowded. Old timers agree, however, that—"you wouldn't know the old place now."

The walls have been decorated by an artist whose imagination must have gone off on a spree. You'll see the wickedest characters leering at you from the murals as well as a bevy of femmes fatale. All in all, the place has been made up to look like an Oppenheimer plot with international intrigue the basis of the motif. Go take a look. You'll be startled—if not scared stiff.

In prewar days the Main could boast—if they felt so inclined—of several flossy bordells. One was located halfway up the hill between Ontario and Sherbrook and catered to the more boisterous show people.

One night an act playing The Lido went on a wild and wooly evening which wound up in the joint. One of the boys in the act spotted a sweet, young chick freshly arrived from the country and promptly fell madly in love.

A council of war was called the following afternoon in Liggett's at the Ford where all concerned tried to bring the boy back to his senses. But to no avail ,as they say in books. He was in love. That was it.

After a solid hour of argument the council of war retreated to the Travelers' Club just off the lobby where, fortified by many drinks, we reasoned with the love-sick actor.

He finally drew himself up, downed his drink and bid us a cheery farewell. We all knew where he was going but didn't feel in the mood to follow. However, a few days later, we received a wire from New York saying that he had upped and married the gal. They are now living in New York and if you know a happier couple—we certainly don't.

The Main in those days was noted for its niteries and the tray toters who served the stupor suds thereabouts. The Val d'Or had a collection of waiters who could serve a party of six with one hand and coolly heave out a drunk with the other.

Among the more famous were a pair of brothers—Harry and Bill Miller. Both were powerful six-footers who became a vital part of Montreal's night life.

Bill, the elder brother, worked a dozen spots around the town before opening a barbequed chicken parlor on Sherbrooke Street. He had beaten his way around the world several times before returning to Montreal.

The day he landed home, loaded with loot, he went out on the town with yours truly and told us his plan of opening a fabulous restaurant. The celebration lasted for some ten days and each succeeding day found Bill telling of opening lesser and lesser eateries as the elastic on the bankroll became progressively looser.

Finally, on the tenth day, Bill decided to go to work and postpone all plans for his restaurant until the bankroll grew back to its former proportions.

He worked at the Hollywood, the American Grill,

the Val d'Or and several other spots before opening the Sherbrooke Street chicken place which he called The Hut.

He was a powerful man—he still is—and, when necessary, his fists could work like pistons. One night at the old Press Club on Phillip's Square, he was laid out by a pair of hoodlums who had terrorized the town for years. Before the cops could carry away the baddies Bill picked himself off the floor and sung a haymaker at the tougher of the two which put the latter to sleep.

When last heard of, he was running a restaurant known as the Blue Center Shop on Monkland Boulevard, He is a walking encyclopedia as far as Montrealia is concerned and, though he has mellowed with the years, it is not considered wise to try pushing him around.

Brother Harry is another who can handle his dukes, although he was not so flamboyant a character as his elder brother. Harry worked the old Montmartre Club at the cor ner of Clark and St.Kit's and had—in fact, he still has—a habit of chewing matches.

He has a mania for renting apartments, furnishing them with the finest material available—then moving. In recent years he has been serving suds at Slitkins and the Bellevue Casino. He is now the headwaiter at the Corso Pizzeria on St. Kit's near St. Dominique.

Another famous character who worked as a waiter at the old Val d'Or was Gaston Lortie. A slender, dark, and fast-talking individual, Lortie had the reputation of getting you anything you wanted at any time of the day or night. He gathered a terrific following and was riding at the peak of popularity when, for some reason or another, he upped and joined the army.

Sent overseas, he finally wound up in the Intelligence and—if you were a war correspondent—you must have recognized him as the sergeant attached to the Press Corps. At present he has a thriving rooming house business and, as far as we know, the last place in which he carried a menu was the El Patio.

Probably the most famous of all graduates of the Val d'Or's serving staff is Albert "The Syrian" Lean, who could carry more drinks on a tray than any two waiters combined.

Lean, also known as "Abdul", was more ambitious than his colleagues. He worked in several spots and, seeing the amount of cabbage that found its way into the cash register, decided that he should get into the business himself.

He did. But not in any amateurish fashion. He gathered himself a partner, Joe Delicatos, also a Val d'Or graduate, and rented a spot on Mountain Street just below Dorchester.

He sunk every dime he could beg or borrow into the place and the result was strictly out of this world. He used an Arabic motif and spent a tidy fortune on water pipes, brass vases, Arabic chairs and other expensive odds and ends. Some of the tables are of inch-thick glass and cost over $200.

For a time, his waiters worked fez-adorned, with a Turkish crescent and wide sashes. He installed a fish pond in the foyer but finally got rid of it after several drunks tried to swim in it. He operated the place, after a lengthy wait for a license, as a late-hour spot and it was an instant success.

He featured shish-kabob and other Syrian dishes and made it his business to know every guest by their first name. As a café operator he had plenty on the ball but a series of tough breaks cost him the club. It was known as The Algiers.

After the collapse of the club, Lean returned to his first love—the carnival. He disappeared for about a year during which Ourtowners received many cards from Port of Prince, Haiti, signed "Abdul."

Just previous to the time this is being written he returned to Montreal driving a block-long convertible and playing the night spots. He is a very heavy tipper and if you hear someone chanting an Arabic song in the background next time you're around a club—chances are that's Abdul.

A flyer for Connie's Inn.
Myron Sutton Scrapbook, Concordia University Archives, S.1p6c

Here Today—
Goniff Tomorrow

IF ANYONE HAD KEPT A RECORD of the night clubs that have opened and closed in Ourtown during the past twenty years, he would have enough material to write an endless series of tear-jerking dramas that would put the current crop of soap operas to shame.

There have been a steady parade of characters with more money than brains buying into night clubs and promptly losing their shirts. Night club business in Montreal is no business for an amateur. The competition is tough and the struggle to keep in operation has caused almost as many stomach ulcers as the stock market.

One of the few inexperienced operators to make money with a club was Adolphe Allard, a butcher from Bonsecours market, who doubled as owner of the now-closed Montmartre club which was located over the Northeastern Lunch on St. Kit's at the Clark Street corner.

Allard, a well-liked young man about town, kept the place fairly packed but found that two businesses were too much for one man. He sold out to Harry Holmok who was then ready for his first night club venture west of Main Street.

Among the more famous waiters at the Montmartre was Albert Langlois, who could open a bottle of champagne in half the time it takes you to pronounce the word.

One night, Langlois gave us our $4.65 change in pennies. We tipped him two hundred pennies in retaliation and he was henceforth known as Penny Langlois. Previously he had been known as Le Sauvage.

The Montmartre changed its policy as often as it changed its table cloths. One of the outstanding headliners to play there was singer Pearl Morris, who later became famous as Mona Morri. When we went to Montreal High School with her we called her Pearl Issenman.

Pearl was a top flight singer. She also spoke flawless French with an accent that stamped her as a Parisian. Once, in Chicago, she applied for, and obtained, the vocalist spot with a name band.

She passed herself off successfully as a recently-arrived French miss and was hired on the spot. During intermissions she had herself a million laughs listening to the conversations of the bandsmen who thought she couldn't speak a word of English.

Following her success in Chicago and New York as Mona Morri, Pearl found herself booked in, of all places, Chez Maurice in Montreal.

She proved a success there and if the home-towners wondered about the strange name—they said nothing. Pearl was singing at the Montmartre the day the dirigible Hindenburg burnt up. She was singing, incidentally, "September in the Rain."

Also to play the Montmartre was a happy couple known to all as the Dancing Hacketts, Frank and Wilma, Pierre and Renée, Kay Lewis—credited with having the loveliest legs in show business and who now lives in Winnipeg—Dusty Rhodes, a Torontonian who quit the

The Canadian Ambassadors, dancers and other
Club Montmartre personnel, October 6, 1937.
*Photo: Roger Janelle. Myron Sutton fonds, Concordia
University Archives, P019-02-08*

business to become a telephone operator in Detroit, and
a Vancouver juggler, Frank Santry, who insisted on living
in Chinatown and eating Chinese food at all hours of
the day and night.

Although many night clubs closed only to re-open
within a short time, the Montmartre closed and stayed
closed. It is now a warehouse for a furniture manu-
facturer.

Albert Lean's Algiers closed but re-opened under the
name of Aldo's. The atmosphere is slightly different from
that of its earlier days but the decorations are still as
lavish.

The spot is now operated by ex-NHL hockey star Jimmy Orlando and his brothers. Jimmy was the former manager of El Morocco and knows most of that which is necessary to know when operating a night club.

If you were writing of his hockey career it would be necessary to type with boxing gloves on because The Orlando on ice is not the quiet, soft-spoken youngster he is when you visit his bistro.

Orlando's career in the NHL is mostly written in liniment. He managed to get into more brawls, bump more opponents on their posteriors and, in general, create more havoc than any other four players in the league.

After leaving the Detroit Red Wings he joined up with the Royals in the Quebec Senior League and blissfully continued his pastime of bumping all and sundry opposition around the rink. His bloodied likeness once appeared as *Life Magazine*'s Picture of the Week. The shot showed Jimmy being pulled from the ice after doing his best to take an entire hockey team apart single-handed.

But that is not the Jimmy Orlando you'll meet at Aldo's. Here, in his nitery, he is the soul of gentleness and does his best to uphold the high ideals which his fan club (it's not generally known—but there is one) credits him with.

Jimmy brought the club into the respectable bracket and it was no easy job. There were many disreputable characters around the place and shooting them out took a great deal of tact, courage and know-how. Today the place is the common meeting ground of actors, musicians, chorus girls, waiters, business men, sightseers, tourists, newspapermen and others of varied callings and professions. But mostly it is a show people's rendezvous. It's here that the hams meet the eggs and the would-be's meet the has-beens.

At time of writing, the Perry Carman Trio is tune-supplying the house, and if you have yet to hear this out-fit, we would strongly suggest you waste no time in doing so. They have been around the town since they were kids and their music is highly listenable.

If you are a fireman—or would like to be, and who wouldn't like to be?—you can meet Johnny Orlando almost any night in the club, providing you get there early enough—he goes to bed early.

Johnny has been a fireman on the Montreal beat for many years and has a host of fellow-firemen from below the border dropping in to talk over various ways and means of eating smoke with or without seasoning.

If you get him in the mood, Johnny will thrill you to bits with his descriptions of various blazes Montreal has witnessed in the past.

Other Orlandos you will likely meet at the spot are Jose, who married Rusty, one of El Morocco's loveliest chorines, and Frank, a promising young hockey star who made the European trip with Canada's representative team the other year. Frank, incidentally, is Lili St. Cyr's constant escort while she is in town.

The staff at the place will be familiar if you know your Montreal. Senior mixologist is Roland, who gradu-ated from El Morocco's lounge, and Nick Vioca, the waiter who was around Harry Holmok's Vienna Grill for more years than we care to remember.

A steady patron of Aldo's is a portly gent known to all as the Jeli-Roll King. His name is really Nelson Wiseman and he's a part-time manager of prizefighters of dubious ability, and part-time press agent for various night clubs.

Wiseman earned his nickname through his ability to do the Jeli-Roll dance back in the Roaring Twenties. The tag was slapped on him by Texas Guinan who considered Wiseman one of the greatest dancers with whom she had ever had the pleasure. The nickname embarrassed the well-educated Wiseman and has been a thorn in his side ever since.

At one time Wiseman had a promising young Greek wrestler among his collection of third-rate boxers. This Greek, claimed Wiseman, was the world's greatest grunt and groaner and he defied all and sundry to dispute same at any time and at any place, providing the latter had sufficient seating capacity to bring in the required amount of shekels. (Aside to Eddie Quinn: This was before Yvon Robert, believe me).

After eliminating all local competition, the Golden Greek, ably managed by Jeli-Roll, looked for new worlds to conquer. They soon found one south of the border and departed in great haste to Jersey where Wiseman had booked in his Hellenic hot shot.

Upon their arrival, however, Jeli-Roll learned much to his surprise and dismay that all wrestling wasn't conducted along strictly honest lines. His fighter was expected to lose to some stumble-bum in order that a return match could be arranged and the taxpayers would return and see same in overwhelming numbers.

Wiseman broke the sad news to the Golden Greek who protested that he always grappled to win and would not think of besmirching the fair name and the noble art of bone-crushing by doing anything so hateful as throwing a fight. So there.

Finally, after much high pressure talking, Wiseman convinced the matman that it was also pleasant to eat three times per day, and that the hotel had just inaugurated a new ruling whereby they handed guest a list of figures and demanded the guest pay the total. It was a grim fight, Maw, but Wiseman finally had his way.

After many weary hours of coaching in the hotel room, Wiseman finally had his protégé ready to lose in the most convincing manner and the pair set out for what was to be the American debut of Canada's greatest wrestler.

The joint was jammed and Jeli-Roll decided that this was strictly the business for him. Like a veteran actor, he counted the house and found it good and all was well with the world. Almost.

The Greek's opponent had been informed that he was to win this bout with as much color and viciousness as possible but not to make the Greek look too bad as there was a return match being primed as a natural and to act accordingly.

However, the instructions couldn't have been explicit because he soon showed that he intended to take the Greek apart as soon as possible and get the bout over with. Who knows—maybe the guy had a date.

He grappled with the Greek and started throwing rabbit punches, gouging and performing other unfair acts, much to the horror and astonishment of the crowd in general and the Greek in particular.

Soon he had flopped Canada's pride flat on his ample shoulders amid boos and catcalls from the female spectators who were solidly behind the Adonis with the shoulders even though he was then in a horizontal position.

The Greek soon tired of all this foul play and despite the repeated coaching he had received, picked up his opponent and dumped him unceremoniously into the ringside seats. A horrified Wiseman grabbed his boy and beat a hasty exit over the border and to this day avoids that particular town in Jersey. It is rumoured about that the promoters are still looking for him.

There are many yarns concerning the Jeli-Roll being bandied here and about. At one time he held the contract—or one of the contracts—giving him the right to handle the affairs of Danny Webb. He no longer has Webb under contract. If you know the boxing game, you will know why. Wiseman was bamboozled out of that deal in such a manner that any sportsman will agree that the methods used were certainly not in the best interests of the fight game. We know—we were there when it happened.

During the time when Webb's contract was the main topic of discussion along Cauliflower Row, Harold "English Harry" Sheppard, acknowledged as rightful holder, telephoned us at *The Herald* and asked if it was true that we were trying to pick up the contract of Johnny Kotsos, brother of our longtime palsy and Nitecap waiter, Billy Kotsos.

We admitted that we liked young Kotsos' style and

hoped to sign him on the dotted line and, knowing Sheppard held his contract, asked how much he wanted for same. Sheppard replied that he wasn't selling but that he would sell us Danny Webb's contract.

"For how much?" we asked eagerly.

"To you—$12," came the astonishing reply.

Sensing a story, we got full details of the offer and printed some verbatim in our column. For this Webb forgave us.

Some time later, Webb's brother and a young veteran who had guided Webb during his army bouts called us for a conference to discuss clearing Webb's name following a load of confusion which surrounded his temporary retirement from the ring. He, after all, had held the British Empire crown and was one of Canada's most promising pugilists.

The meeting was held in the offices of Tiny Koren on McKay Street when Koren was with the advertising firm of Garber-Cossman. It was a negative affair at best, inasmuch as neither Webb's brother nor his ex-manager told us anything that we did not already know.

We had known for some time that Webb was in hot water with American interests who wanted him to fight under their wing—and he had refused. We knew why Webb wasn't getting the bouts he rated and we also knew that those who chose to disregard the U.S. interests often were found in the alleyway in an advanced state of disrepair.

We took a deep breath and told the meeting that we would print the entire story and therefore clear some of the fog that enveloped Danny Webb. We were held to a promise, however. That promise was to hold the story until given the green light by Webb's brother.

Although this was not our usual procedure, we agreed on the condition that we were to have the story exclu-sive—we already had it—and any harm that might befall all concerned would be relayed to *The Herald* immediately.

After a lengthy three-day wait for the "go" sign, we received a telephone call to forget the whole thing. We refused. But a promise is a promise so the story remained unwritten.

It was over a year before we saw Webb again. This time we were in the Café St. Michel when he entered with a few friends. He gave us a rather cool greeting but we were very used to cool greetings at that time so didn't take time out to wonder about causes for same.

As we were leaving the club, however, we passed Webb on the stairs. A conscientious kid, we figured he would be morally obligated to explain. He did. He resented my column describing the telephone conversation in which his contract was offered for $12!

Whether or not Webb was—or is—aware of the fact that we had offered to stick our necks out on his behalf is beside the point. We had always been in his corner, even during the lengthy period spent overseas.

At that time, yours truly, along with Sgt. Sammy Koffman, were with the daily Maple Leaf. Webb was fighting some British pug, whose name escapes us at the moment, and Koffman and I decided to give our boy the big spread.

We haunted the gym where he worked out and

screamed his praises in letters this high. Came the day of the fight, we ran a full page of pictures and columns of glowing praises and really did the thing up right. We also bet a month's pay on him.

Webb lost the bout and we spent the next month borrowing shillings from Major Jack Goulding and Captain Jack (*Vancouver Sun*) Scott. This wasn't too great a hardship to endure but we often get to wondering if Danny Webb ever knew how many guys were in his corner—apart from the usual seconds.

It might be interesting to note at this time that while the controversy raged over who owned the contract to Danny Webb, *The Herald*'s Sports Editor, Elmer W. Ferguson, gave us a copy of a contract signed and sealed by all concerned, which indignantly listed Danny Webb as being the property of a London fight manager. The contract was made out on the stationary of the British Boxing Commission—which explains why we didn't buy a gold mine with twelve bucks.

The Scrambled-Eared Gentry

YOU DON'T HAVE TO BE a mind reader to realize that Montreal is making a desperate bid to become the continent's number one fight center—as far as the lightweights are concerned. Both The Forum and the ball park have been the scene of some of the greatest battles and the greatest stinkeroos ever to louse up the boxing game.

Most of the credit for bringing the sport into the local limelight is due a gravel-throated French-Canadian known in Montreal sporting circles as Raoul Godbout.

Raoul, along with his brother Philip, operated a night club called The Palermo which was—and still is—situated opposite the stockyards at the corner of Frontenac and Mount Royal Avenue in the northeastern section of the city.

The two brothers ran The Palermo during its heyday as a major league nitery in prewar days. It was here that the Creedon Sisters, Helen Kerns and Rod Rodgers enjoyed their greatest local successes. The spot was the haunt of such well-known localities as Louis "The Kid" Assal and his brother Michael "Prince Mike." A list of the musicians who played there resembles a Who's Who in the music world.

It was here that "Sphinx" Demarais first played Ellington's haunting tune, "In a Sentimental Mood," and it was here that sax-tooter Bob Perrault blew his horn. It was also here that a lovely lassie named Audrey Evraire first enchanted the evenings by singing such songs as "Be Sure It's True" and "J'attendrai."

Audrey later married Charley Kitson, then with Hal Hartley's orchestra, and retired from show business after a brilliant debut. Kitson is still playing piano and is considered one of the top keyboard men in the city. Currently he is teamed with up-and-coming singer Rolly Legault.

Despite the success of The Palermo, Raoul was not content to sit back and watch the lettuce roll in. He was homesick for the sound of the clicking turnstiles and, with that in mind, constructed a pint-sized stadium in the grounds behind the club. He called it the Stade Exchange.

Yours truly was then writing wrestling for the old *L'Illustration Nouvelle* and recalled clearly that some of the wrestling bouts smelled far worse than the stockyards across the street, even when the wind was right.

Raoul, however, had the magic touch. His Stade Exchange proved a gold mine and his next step was to move in on the boxing industry. Today he is top promoter of prize fights in the Dominion and works closely with his distinguished friends and philosophers the Mssrs. Slitkin and Slotkin.

Montreal has produced a few good heavyweights. The accent has definitely been on welters and light-weights. One of the most colorful produced locally is Maxie "The Burglar" Berger.

Maxie graduated from club fights around the local area to a hot-shot attraction at Madison Square Garden.

He is a familiar figure around the local scene and has an admirable sense of loyalty to his mentors, the afore-mentioned firm of Slitkin and Slotkin.

For our money, Maxie is the greatest battler to come out of the old home town since Leo Kid Roy. Berger is a smart boxer, a terrific slugger and has that rare inability to realize that he is licked.

A few years ago ,the YMHA held an Old Timer night in which the leather punching gentry of yesteryear appeared, complete with pot bellies, to throw hooks and crosses against opponents with similar pot bellies.

All except Maxie. The Burglar was matched against a smart young battler who fought under the name of Sammy Jacobs. This kid was no old timer. He was young, ambitious and packed dynamite in each fist.

For some reason or other, we got ourselves mixed up in the deal by agreeing to second Maxie in his bout. Knowing Maxie as long as we had, we knew that he was definitely not in shape. We figured that Jacobs would cut the old warhorse to pieces.

To add to our concern, we learned that Jacobs had been practicing a left hook for some three weeks and was all keyed up to throw same at our bosom pal. Realizing that Maxie was a sucker for a left hook, we were not at all happy when we climbed into his corner armed with the usual water bottle and towel.

During the first round, we were wondering if, by hocking our watch and typewriter, we could raise enough loot to purchase Jacobs' contract. The kid was slightly colossal. He worried The Burglar, who seemed to have trouble finding a target. He danced around the ring like

Dauthieulle, threw body punches like Greco and slugged it out with all the Griffintown technique of Gus Mell.

A dozen times we thought Maxie had had it. But Berger walked to the corner at the end of the round, took the water bottle from our hands and insisted on fanning us with the towel. He was playing it smart.

At the same time, we were aging at a very rapid rate waiting for Jacobs to throw a left hook. About four seconds along in the second round, he did. It caught The Burglar on the chin and he stepped back in a hurry, blowing through his flattened nose with all the ferocity of Ferdinand The Bull. Then he jabbed his left like a souped up streak of lightning, catching Jacobs unprepared.

He followed with a series of lefts and rights and the kid was soon bouncing on the ropes like a yo-yo. If anyone around the ringside that night had any doubts but that Maxie Berger was a terrific battler—their doubts were dispelled in the greatest exhibition of fisticuffs it has been this writer's privilege to watch—and we have watched many ring battles.

Anyone with less guts than Jacobs would have quit cold. But the kid stayed in there and fought it out. For some reason or other he quit the ring soon after thereby depriving Canada of a promising young hopeful.

The bout is still discussed around ring circles. If you ever run into Ann Fishman, then a reporter on the [Canadian] Jewish Eagle, or Dave Miller, then swimming coach at the YMHA, they will tell you of the famous bouts between Maxie Berger and the young'un Sammy Jacobs.

Maxie operated a tailor shop on Beaver Hall Hill for a short while, then became the official meeter and greeter at a Peel Street night club. Today he has an establishment on Mansfield Street and will sell you custom-made shirts and, if you're interested, will give you the lowdown on the fight game or go out and have coffee and conversation with you. He is a very solid citizen.

In Montreal, Maxie Berger is considered the standard by which every boxer to come up since has been judged. The most colorful since Berger is a young, blond battler known as Gus "Pell" Mell, a product of Griffintown and a very handy gent with his dukes, to say the least.

However, Mell is unpredictable. He is strictly a street brawler who regards training as boring, a way in which to pass the time. He is the most unassuming person we have ever met. It's all so simple with Gus. If he doesn't feel in the mood to train—he doesn't train.

We once lost $400 on one of his fights. We have lost a bit more coin of the realm on his battles since but this particular fight sticks in our memory like a hook in a catfish's gullet.

We had heard rumors that Gussie wasn't training. That he had a stomach like a pregnant pup. That he was as out of shape as a pair of high-button shoes and that it would be financial suicide to lay a bet on him.

Somehow we smothered our better judgement and laid the bet taking the short odds. After all, Pell Mell was unpredictable and there was still a chance that the management of the Ford Hotel would give us a decent credit rating and we wouldn't be forced to sleep with the pigeons in Dominion Square.

Came fight night and Mell crawled through the ropes looking as if he had spent three weeks on a Roman orgy.

His stomach bulged over his tights and he looked ready for a Turkish bath rather than a prize fight.

It was not surprising that he lost the fight. But, at the same time, he made such a showing that we just couldn't find ourselves taken. He put up a great fight— he always does—and provided more color to the card than any other bout.

We readily admit that we have lost more money betting on Mell than we have on any other fighter. But there is something about the kid that intrigues us. He is a courageous battler. He's a terror when he's on. Regardless of his condition, he can bring the house down with his unorthodox method of slugging it out. No Fancy Dan he. One day he is going to take his boxing seriously. When that day comes we will gain a very clever boxer—but will probably lose a very colorful one.

For our money, the smartest fisticuffer, both in and out of the ring, is a young pae-san who has a weaving, slugging style which baffles opponents. He is Johnny Greco, the pride of Notre Dame de Grace and the terror of his division.

Greco is reaching the end of his boxing career, but unlike so many leather pushers ,he has few worries about the future. Smart management and shrewd judgement assures the walloping Roman of a steady income when he has put away the gloves.

Midnight Manners

IF YOU ARE GOING OUT for an evening on the town, leave the family jalopie at home. Parking space is a rare thing indeed and local courts are very rough on drunken drivers. Besides, taxis are both plentiful and cheap. And what's more, you'll probably get the biggest thrill of the evening driving in one. Montreal cabbies are a race apart. There isn't one who couldn't qualify as a Hell Driver. They'll get you where you want to go—but fast. If you have a weak heart, tell the driver before you start out.

You may get away with wearing your hat in a bar in Toronto or New York but don't try it in Montreal—it just isn't done. It is customary to check your top piece or—better still—don't wear one.

Formal dress is absolutely out, unless you are going to a posh affair which insists on same. This goes for gals as well as guys. If you wear a tux, you're liable to be mistaken for a waiter, and if you're a gal, an evening dress will probably set all and sundry to thinking that you are part of the floor show. It is conspicuous and, besides, it is uncomfortable.

Always wear a tie and jacket evenings, though the heat is killing you. Some places insist you wear a coat; if you don't happen to be wearing one they will supply you with a light, tropical jacket. Both Café Martin and the Indian Room will loan you a coat. See the headwaiter.

Montrealers are quietly sophisticated. This is not a town you "tear up" on a night out. (Aside to Torontonians: Don't snicker, Mister. The only persons who ever tore up your town are the boys digging the subway).

Don't get the idea that chorus girls are there for the express purpose of keeping you company. There is a union law which permits them to mix but only when and with whom they choose. Most have boy friends and it is always advisable to find out first if they are attached. Otherwise, you may find yourself buying drinks like mad for the babe, only to have her say a cheerful good night after the last show and link her arm with her one and only, leaving you dismayed and holding a sizeable tab. Far better to look—but don't touch.

If you're dating a waitress don't try to impress her with the importance of your job. She probably makes more money than you do. Let her choose the spot for dinner. If you are a liberal tipper, she will steer you to a place where she knows a few colleagues. If she does, tip heavily—no use making the doll look bad in front of her friends.

If you are loaded with loot and want to make an impression on your date, start the afternoon off with cocktails at the Indian Room. You'll find the prices reasonable, despite the lavish surroundings. Then drive out to Ruby Foo's on the Sunset Strip. Food, music and drinks are just about the best you'll find in the city at this elaborate spot. As long as you are in a French town, you may as well eat French food so try Léo Dandurand's Café Martin on Mountain Street. The Flamingo Room is perfect for light conversation in case you're planning on pitching a proposition.

Would suggest that you next take in the show at either the Bellevue Casino or the Folies Bergères. You can take in both during the course of an evening without too much scrambling around. If she looks good enough to eat—she probably does frequently—so spare ribs at the Chic-N-Coop would be in order.

If she goes for serious jazz, you can walk her from the Chic-N-Coop to Ciro's in about two minutes and let the chick get her kicks to some of the finest jive available in town. Next stop is naturally Aldo's, where she can show off—or vice versa—to almost everyone else out on dates that night.

If there is a floor show in the club, slip your head-waiter two bucks if there are two of you. Five bucks if there are four. Give the busboy at least a half buck and your waiter at least two more. If you can't afford these prices—stay at home. Standard tip for both a hat chick or a hackie is a quarter.

If your date wants to dance, beg off if possible. Only dopes dance and some of the kids terpsi you bow-legged if you're not careful.

Don't whistle your appreciation for the floor show. Don't hammer your glass with a swizzle stick. If you're not hep to show business, wait until someone else applauds before doing so or you're liable to make a noise at the wrong time and earn the undying hatred of the act on stage.

Don't order dinner unless you have enough time to finish it before the show starts. Don't talk while an act is on. Don't pass wise cracks—regardless of how witty they may seem—at the show girls. You're likely to get launched with a bottle over the head.

If you're a New Yorker, don't try to give your date that Big Town deal about how fast Manhattan is. She has probably been in your home town and knows that you can't drink after four bells in the morning unless you know someone who will steer you to an oasis. Far better you should realize right off that Montreal is a faster town as far as drinkeries are concerned, regardless of how bitter a pill that is to swallow. If you're from Toronto—just keep quiet and no one will know the difference.

Montrealers love to talk about Montreal. So if you know a bit about the city, you get a far better rating with your guest if you talk about the town than you will if you speak of greater, downtown, metropolitan Simmons' Corners, Saskatchewan. If you don't like Montreal, keep it to yourself—there are trains, ships and planes leaving it every day. Most of all, don't insult the Metropolis within earshot of your date or she, in most cases, will get up and leave you sitting by your lonesome.

Bienvenue, Mon Vieux

IF YOU ARE ONE OF THOSE PERSONS who wants to live permanently in Montreal—and who isn't?—you'll find that you'll get along much easier if you speak French. Regardless of how badly you do, you'll soon discover that the average French-Canadian appreciates your efforts with his language and will help you conquer the tongue. While few English-speaking residents ever bother to learn French, most French-Canadians are bilingual.

Gals who wish to live in the big town should first save a bit of money. Don't get enthusiastic over newspaper want ads that advertise for waitresses or models. Montreal is filled with first-class tray toters and models and chances are the advertiser is looking for some stranded chick who will, in desperation, take anything offered. And what he has to offer you can find in your own home town.

It's wise to spend your first night in town at a hotel. Get up early and go hunting for a more or less permanent place to live. First ask your waitress if she knows of a place. Most of these gals live in rooms or apartments in the uptown district and can steer you to a decent place or know of someone who can.

If you are running a single harness and have a steady doll, she'll expect you to take her out on Tuesdays, Thursdays and Saturdays. Those are sweetheart nights in Montreal. If you are in the lower income bracket, she'll expect you to night club her only on Saturday nights. This will give you four nights per week to go wolfing on your own or to go out drinking with the boys. If you are looking for male company try the bowling alleys or Mother Martin's. You'll find a lot of guys at these places who are in the same spot as you and who, like yourself, would like to make a few friends for the odd poker game or fishing trip.

If you are a Communist—keep out of Quebec. This is no place for the disciples of Marx, Lenin and (you should pardon the expression) Josef Stalin. This is a Roman Catholic province and Communism is not welcome. Premier Maurice Duplessis, more than any other Canadian premier, has done more to combat the Red menace using methods which, you may think, are dictatorial but which you must admit, are effective.

If you are a Witness of Jehovah and plan to see copies of *The Watchtower* on Montreal streets—think again. You're most likely to wind up in the hoosegow. Montreal had a session with the Witnesses which should settle all doubts as to the province's attitude towards them.

It seems that several hundred were arrested recently and lodged in the local clink where they remained until bailed out by restaurateur, Frank Roncarelli. Roncarelli, at the time, operated the Crescent Street café bearing his name and also The Quaff Club, which occupied the basement of the premises.

Somehow or other the cafe and bar were closed and Roncarelli sued like mad. The case is still being fought out in the local courts but it is a significant fact that Jehovah's Witnesses have disappeared from the streets.

The Demi-Monde

MONTREAL HAS HAD SOME very hard characters who passed as citizens. One of the toughest was a very young lumberjack whose name was doubled barreled—Girard Girard.

One of Girard's favorite methods of earning a living was to walk up to a nearby passerby and simply relieve him of every dime he carried. He had a few gals working for him in the district and his fame soon spread up and down the Tenderloin.

One night while he was idling outside Dave's Delicatessen at Clark and St. Kit's, he saw a cop walking in great haste toward him. From his vantage point, he noted that the boy in blue was at least six foot and therefore his chin was rather out of reach for anyone who stood a mere five-foot, four inches.

Girard rushed in to the delicatessen and borrowed a chair which he placed in the middle of the sidewalk and climbed upon it. From his vantage point on the chair, he waited until the cop came into range, then threw an uppercut which, eyewitnesses swear, lifted the policeman at least two feet off the ground. Girard then made himself scarce.

About a week later, he was spotted relieving a citizen of his bankroll on Berger Street and was chased by two patrolmen. He ran through the entrance of a delicatessen on St. Kit's, near City Hall Avenue, but was shot before he reached the kitchen. The coppers breathed a sigh of relief as the body was moved to the morgue and the name Girard Girard became a mere memory.

Strangely enough, Girard, as tough as he was, was scared stiff by Fred Zarbotiny. Zarbotiny at that time was running a café called The Little Egypt on St. Lawrence Main and was the only character in town who could handle the pugnacious lumberjack.

Zarbotiny was later found dead in a fire and his restaurant passed to different hands, but he is well remembered by those who were around at the time as the guy who could have tamed Girard Girard had he had the chance.

Girard, of course, was not considered a typical example of a Montreal gangster. He was uncouth, unshaven and strictly a mass of muscle with little grey matter to back up his lethal fists.

On the other hand, Tony Frank and his mob were exact opposites. Tough, polished, impeccably clad, they constituted Montreal's first group of racketeers as we know them today. All were hanged at Bordeaux Jail following the fatal Hochelaga armed car holdup.

One of the most dangerous of the mob was known as Dago Frank, who was reputed to have been involved in the "Rosy" Rosenthal murder in New York. Others were Serafini, Valentino and a young, good-looking hood known as Chitchi Gambino.

Gambino came up from New York and settled easily into the casual atmosphere of Montreal's underworld. He soon owned and operated a brothel on Desmarais

Street and was figured as being a deputy crime minister in the town.

He was also carrying the biggest torch this side of the Statue of Liberty for a gal who used the name of Kate Mansfield and who was a soubrette at the old Starland Theater. Their romance was a beautiful thing to behold inasmuch as the whole town was scared stiff of Gambino and Gambino was scared stiff of Kate.

One night the entire mob was whooping it up at the old Bouillon Hotel on the corner of St. Dominique and St. Kit's when Gambino entered with a face so long he had three tongues in his shoes. Seems as though he and Kate had been battling and he was a very morbid soul indeed.

Gambino had a quaint habit of concealing stilettos up his sleeves so arranged that, when he hugged anyone, they pierced the flesh. He was wearing this pleasant arrangement the night he tangled with Richardson and in no time whatsoever Richardson was being stabbed by Gambino's bear hung and the blood flowed like wine.

Several patrons of the spot who attempted to interfere in the matter were pushed aside by various members of Frank's mob. Finally Valentino pulled out a huge Colt .45 and threatened to blast the first guy who stuck his nose into what wasn't his affair.

Meanwhile Sammy Vineberg came out from the kitchen, sized up the situation and jumped Valentino, gun and all.

This happened shortly before the Tony Frank gang pulled the Hochelaga bank robbery, which resulted in the greatest mass hanging Montreal has known.

Tony Frank's funeral was the flossiest affair the town had seen. Neatly tucked away in a solid copper casket Montreal's first big-time gangster was paid final homage by thousands of citizens who regarded him as a Robin Hood. He wasn't. He was merely a tough boy who didn't know enough to quit when he was on top.

No one ever came even close to Tony Frank as a top ranking mobster in town. A few have tried but the town just couldn't be bothered. Gangsters can stand anything but ridicule. Anyone who knows the inside of the Roy Castleman fiasco will know what we mean.

A few years ago, Castleman was a disc jockey broadcasting from night clubs in Montreal and had occasion to rub his padded shoulders with the hoi polloi of Montreal's gangdom. Somehow the discker wasn't impressed.

During his latter days as a platter spinner, there was much talk about a "million-dollar" layout at a gambling joint nearby. All concerned were very much impressed, except Castleman. He ridiculed the rackoes and called them—but right out loud—a bunch of tin horns and went just as far as it is possible to go over the airways.

One night a pair of muscled gents walked into the club to have a few words with Castleman. They stood in the entrance to the dining room and glared at the kid. To Castleman's credit let us state at this moment that, although he missed his cue, he certainly wasn't scared.

He looked the two mobsters straight in the eye and started talking about—of all things—the supposedly "million-dollar" layout they were operating.

"Since when," said Castleman, "do two crap tables and a broken-down roulette wheel constitute a million-dollar layout?" For some reason or other, his broadcast was canceled and Montreal lost the first hep disc jockey it had known to that date.

Who's Brew?

DESPITE AN ARGUMENT that may be advanced by the few remaining Drys, the fact remains that the brewing business contributes greatly to the national income of Montreal.

The brewing industry is the fourth largest in the city and employs some 2,000 persons. Its capital ranges near the thirty-million-dollar mark and its produce is appreciated by localites in general and American tourists in particular.

Maisonneuve granted a license to a brewer when the town was still known as Ville Marie. Before that the citizens drank spruce beer—an antidote to scurvy—and a drink which you may still find in the town if you look hard enough.

The first brewery on record was built by Jesuit Father Lejeune at Sillery, Quebec, 'round about 1646. In 1650 Jean Talon encouraged brewing of beer, which he considered a more temperate drink than brandy or rum, and arranged for wholesale planting of hops for a state-controlled brewery.

In 1672 the city got into the act and started a brewery with funds borrowed from the Gentlemen of Saint-Sulpice. Charles le Moyne, Seigneur de Longueuil, erected a brew house near the fort of Montreal in 1690. In 1704 the Reverend Brothers Charon built a brewery in Point St. Charles.

By the time the eighteenth century rolled in, Montreal had six breweries and a steady demand for suds keeping them all busy. In 1786 John Molson established his first. This is the oldest one on the North American continent and is still being operated by his descendents.

Molson was the first of Canada's industrialists. The name is respected wherever Canadians gather and it may be well to note at this time that one of his descendents, Colonel John Molson, is a brilliant military figure who wears the colors of the famed Black Watch.

Back in the early days of the brewery, beer sold for nine cents—if you preferred the strong stuff—and seven cents if you preferred the milder ale. A table of beer cost five cents and beer drinkers today will envy the old, old timers who could quaff the stuff at those prices.

Dawes Black Horse Brewery was started in Lachine in 1811 but was later moved to Montreal. Dow's Brewery was first located in Laprairie and moved to Montreal in 1808. These two breweries, along with seven other Montreal firms and a few from other parts of the province, merged in 1909 under the name of National Breweries.

It is National Breweries that puts out Frontenac Blue Label which, for our money anyway, is the greatest beer ever brewed. However, that's only our opinion. The most popular beer served locally is Molson's. U.S. tourists go for it in a big way and it is "the long green bottle" that is seen on most tables around the town.

During the war, Molson's ale was a rare commodity indeed. Places with a goodly stock soon found that thirsty customers went through the supply in no time whatsoever.

A rather good friend of ours operated a broken-down bistro near Criminal Court at that time and was constantly plagued by customers who insisted on being served Molson's—and nothing else.

As the demand far exceeded the supply, he devised a plan whereby he kept everybody happy. First he obtained an old fashioned boiler which he cut in half. This he filled with hot water and then placed bottles of an inferior brand of beer therein. As soon as the labels became unstuck, he replaced same with Molson labels and served the beer as Molson's.

At first customers complained that the beer didn't taste like Molson's. This, he explained was due to the ancient vintage. In time the taxpayers grew accustomed to the taste of this inferior beer masquerading as the real stuff and told all within earshot that they knew of a place which served genuine Molson's.

Our pal did all right for himself during the war years and collected huge handfuls of beautiful greenbacks. However, as soon as the war was over and Molson's got back into something akin to normal production, his customers complained that he was trying to pull a fast one when he served them the genuine Molson's beer. They were so used to the taste of the inferior stuff they swore that a Molson wasn't a Molson.

You can order beer from your grocer's in Montreal. It costs slightly more than a quarter a quart and you may be forced into ordering a load of groceries when you want only beer. If this happens—try another store. There is no shortage of beer today, although some groceries will try to convince you that there is.

Incidentally, you need not feel inferior if you order

beer in a night club in Montreal. Most people drink the stuff rather than hard liquor. If you stick to one brand, chances are you will escape a hangover the following day. But don't try to mix Quebec beer with spirits or you'll wake up with a taste that will convince you that you've been chewing Indonesian wrestler's trunks—and that's for sure.

Label celebrating Dow Brewery's 150th anniversary, 1940.
Frank Mrazik Collection

Montreal's People

THERE IS LITTLE DOUBT that Scotsmen form a solid backbone in Montreal's business world. In 1937 the brilliant French author, Andrew Siegried, wrote "in the telephone directory there are six pages of MACS. Tear them out and Montreal is no longer a financial capital but an immense French village with a little English garrison."

In later years, Sir Wilfred Laurier, speaking at a St. Andrew's Day banquet, quoted a prayer attributed to Canada's Scottish fur traders which ran thusly: "O Lord, we do not ask you to give us wealth, but show us where it is."

The Scots got a toe hold on the fur business and have held on since. The traditional friendship between France and Scotland helped the merchants in the early days when so much depended upon the French-Canadian voyageur canoe men who brought in the furs.

Montreal's blue book reads like an Aberdeen city directory. The most important social event of the year is the St. Andrew's Ball held yearly at the Windsor Hotel.

The ball was first held in 1878 and officially opened the Windsor Hotel. It has been held yearly ever since then, with time out for a couple of wars.

Any deb with social aspirations, who lacks a bid to this affair, will find her career set back no end. The Ball also gives the gay young blades the opportunity of wearing those plaid pants known as "trews." It's quite a clam-bake indeed.

Comes March the seventeenth and the Wearin of the Green and Montreal becomes a small bit of Erin. The annual St. Patrick's Day Parade brings out marchers with such un-Hiberian handles as Arsenault, Archambault and Lepine—as well as those who spring from the Auld Sod.

The Harps arrived here in great numbers in 1821 and the years following. It seemed that the potato crop nose-dived in Ireland and mass unemployment followed the Napoleonic Wars thereby giving the government a hard time.

To offset the famine and distress they encouraged Irishmen to kiss the Blarney Stone farewell and go to Canada. Most were slated for farms in the Upper St. Lawrence but a great many of them never got past Montreal.

They settled in an area in the south-western section of Point St. Charles. The land was subdivided into building lots by a young Irishman named Griffin. The section, therefore, became known as Griffintown.

Although they didn't create any financial history—most arrived without a dime—they moved into politics and dominated them. They intermarried with the French-Canadians like mad. They still do. They soon learned the language, and even today you'll note that the average Harp speaks fluent French. Unlike their neighbors back home, the Irish and the Scots, the English do not merge as easily in the French atmosphere. Many cling to the bonds of Empire and are reluctant to let go.

Some have an air of superiority about them and manage to make themselves as popular as a skunk at a garden party. Others resent the fact that French is the main language and make no effort to learn it.

Others simply eat their hearts out for Over 'Ome and there are few who do not make the trip back providing they have the money. The majority settle down to a peaceful life in the city and their children usually grow up without the prejudices of their parents.

Their attitude toward the French is changing rapidly. This is best explained by the number of English war brides the French-Canadian troops brought home with them.

However, there is still some friction between some French-Canadians and some English-Canadians. Those who deny the fact don't know their Montreal. While other races refer to themselves as being English-Canadians and Irish-Canadians, the French-Canadian refers to himself as being a "Canadien." His is the only nationality to do so.

It is all very well for the do-gooders to point out examples of National Unity and proclaim to all within earshot that all is sweetness and light between the two races—but the fact remains that there is a common resentment.

There are approximately 30,000 Italians living in the city. Most live in the northern section of the town, with St. Hubert and Bélanger streets forming the main intersection.

The pae'sans also have an elaborate club house known as the Casa d'Italia—which the city paid for and which the army took over during the war.

The Casa was well known for its Thursday night spaghetti-and-dance sessions and for its superior athletic products. Some of the best amateur ball players are Italians.

The colony borders closely on the Syrian district, which huddles around the corner of St. Denis and Bélanger. This section was the spawning ground for the mobsters, who dominated the gambling scene when Montreal had a gambling scene.

It was in this district that the short-lived numbers racket originated. It was the brain child of a grocer who got tired of selling beans and went out after the heavy loot but was also back selling beans when the town just didn't go for the numerical game.

The 1941 census revealed that there were 713,522 French-Canadians and 159,669 English Canadians living in the town. Other races brought the total up to 1,139,921. The census also listed 839,084 Roman Catholics, 103,270 Anglicans, 50 Mormons and 1,227 Confucians and Buddhists.

All in all, it's a very cosmopolitan town. You can get indigestion in any language—the town is loaded with restaurants. You can pray under any type of architecture you choose and, if you ask around a bit, you're sure to find a colony of fellow-countrymen, even if you are an Eskimo.

Skid Row

MONTREAL'S STREET OF LOST CAUSES in that strip of Craig Street [now St. Antoine]which extends eastwards from Bleury to Place Viger Square. It is lined, as every Skid Row in the world is lined, with cheap flop houses. Here, for a dime, you can get a place to sleep off a drunk without bothering anybody but the bedbugs.

Some of the joints call themselves hotels and charge two bits for a bed. There is quite a bit of social distinction between those who check into the two-bit joints and those who must settle for the less pretentious ten-cent inns.

It is doubtful that you can walk forty feet along this strip without being bummed for a dime. It's far better to cough up fifteen cents than to get the frigid look bestowed upon those who only donate a mere dime to a fellow human.

If the bum looks a bit plastered, don't stop. Just walk as fast as possible or you'll be in for rough time. Chances are he's a "rubby-dub" and his mind is no doubt clouded with smoke. These types are quite capable of creating quite a row if you're offering is not up to his expectations. And it seldom is.

Strangely enough, there are few "winos" in Montreal. While getting foozled on cheap vintage is the thing to do among Toronto's flotsam and jetsam, it is considered vulgar by the Montreal set.

Favorite drink along Craig Street is rubbing alcohol mixed with vanilla extract. Some druggists refuse to sell the stuff to anyone they think will take it internally. However, there is little apparent difficulty in obtaining it, judging by the number of crocked carcasses you'll see sleeping it off in the doorways.

Some favor shoe polish heated and strained through cotton. This potent drink has been known to cause almost instant blindness. However, this risk is not considered to be great by many who point out that a tin cup and a handful of pencils are easily obtained.

Unlike other less fortunate Skid Rows, Montreal's boasts of a summer residence. It is that strip of land on the canal banks near the Point St. Charles. Here the bums congregate to drink and to discuss world events. Every now and then one rolls into the canal but no one seems to mind, unless of course, he forgot to let go the bottle before hitting the water. The police department has probably given up keeping score of the number of rubbies they have fished out of the river—some dead, some living, but all thoroughly soaked.

In recent years, Craig Street has been undergoing a face lifting. Several new buildings and many new store fronts have replaced depressing edifices. Pawnshops still dominate the street and you can buy anything from a military medal to a violin or gun on the north side of the thoroughfare.

The Broken Leg Brigade

EVERY WINTER WEEKEND, thousands of Montrealers climb into ski togs, grab their barrel staves and head for the North Country. Every summer weekend they grab their swim suits and do the same thing. The only time of the year Montrealers are not heading north is that frustrating period when there is not enough snow on which to ski and the other depressing time when it is too cold to swim.

Otherwise, it's a mass shuffle which blocks the roads and jampacks the trains. Ste. Agathe is a mere sixty miles and is considered the heart of the North Country.

Although it seems rather strange to go sixty miles to break a leg when Mount Royal offers splendid ski trails where you can get busted up without having to leave the city.

However, the thing to do is to go "Up North." The Laurentians are dotted with hotels and lodges ranging all the way from broken down shacks to super-swanky inns where you will be expected to change clothes about six times a day and please wear your jacket at meal times.

Some, notably the Manor House, feature floor shows starring acts from Montreal night clubs. They also have a comic who is considered unofficial Night Mayor of the Mountains. He is Jackie Kahane who, a few years ago, was a druggist's clerk. He soon found he had more fun gagging with customers than he did actually selling aspirins—so he became a comic.

He has been at the Manor House for a few seasons and takes time out for night club dates only when the mountains go through the waiting periods between skiing and swimming.

Almost every Montreal has a favorite spot in the mountains. Some head as far north as they can possibly go while others merely drive seventeen miles to Ste. Rose where there are night clubs on every corner.

Ski parties constitute the greatest excuse to get out of town in the winter. Gangs of guys and gals get rigged up in slacks and heavy boots away from deep snows. Most stock up heavily on refreshments and soon get into such a state that they don't know, or particularly care, where or why they're going. At these types of gatherings, you can leave your skis at home—no one will know the difference.

Others take their skiing seriously and will talk at great length about slaloms and other strange accomplishments. The sport has boomed in recent years and if a mountain lodge is not equipped with a ski-tow it is frowned upon by the skiing fraternity.

If you're planning on staying in the mountains during the summer, it is always wise to make plenty of enquiries before choosing a lodge. Some are veddy, veddy formal, and unless you have an extensive wardrobe, you'll feel like a tramp. Even if you have, you may not appreciate climbing in and out of it as often as the lodge-keeper expects.

The younger crowd have, in recent years, flocked to a place called Parkdale on Lac L'Achigan. Eaton's Summer Camp is also on this lake, which may explain its sudden popularity.

Also on Lac L'Achigan is Jules Racicot's rambling summer lodge, where guests are served by uniformed butlers and all is dignified and plushy.

Newspapermen invariably go to Auberge de Sèvre, also on Lac L'Achigan. De Sevre's is an informal lodge with plenty of dancing space and two bars. Probably the coolest bar in the mountains is located in the basement of the main house.

There are hundreds of first-class spots within easy driving distance of Peel and St. Kit's, and, if you are a stranger, you won't remain one long in this area. It's probably the friendliest hunk of land in Canada.

It has long been the habit of those driving up North to stop at St. Jerome for a drink. If you are driving, it's wise to stick to lemonade because the highway north of St. Jerome is the greatest speedway this side of Indianapolis.

Time was when this road was a dirt path on which two wagons could barely pass without locking wheels. Now, thanks to man's engineering genius, it is a super highway where six cars can collide in a fatal accident and still have room to spare.

On a summer Sunday afternoon you'll pass the dead and dying and the battered cars and automatically drive slowly. One look at the wrecks and you'll make a mental promise to yourself to take it easy at the wheel.

If you are a member of the horsy set, you'll find some high-grade horseflesh at St. Thérèse Lodge just over the bridge from St. Rose. This is an all-year-round resort and is easily accessible, regardless of the weather.

Montreal, although surrounded by water, hasn't a beach. If you want to know the reason you'll have to read some other book. We don't know why—therefore we can't tell you. Every summer the old question is asked regarding the lack of swimming facilities on the Island and every fall finds the question unanswered.

Editors can always count on an avalanche of mail from readers who wonder why the city doesn't do something about it. Editorial writers can always view with alarm our beach-less Island when editorial writing lags through lack of something to editorialize about.

The fact remains that the Island doesn't have a beach. At one time a group of New Yorkers planned to build a little Coney Island on Nun's Island, which lies just off Verdun. Nothing came of the idea, and Montreal still doesn't have a beach.

There are two good indoor pools, however. One is in Verdun and is considered one of the finest in the Dominion. A Wellington Street car will get you almost there. Leave your suntan lotion at home and don't smoke once you're in. It's taboo.

The other is on the Sunset Strip, as Decarie Boulevard is called, in Ville St. Laurent. It is operated by George Gavaris, who has the Astor Grill on St. Kit's.

The pool is part of a drive-in restaurant on the highway and is the favorite afternoon sunning spot for chorus gals. You'll see some superb shapes around the pool ,and if you decide to swim, you'll find the water well-filtered and just the right temperature.

Don't go swimming in the Back River or the St. Lawrence. The former is probably polluted and the latter is oily. Besides, you are liable to be nudged by a tug boat or an ocean liner.

There are several indoor public pools scattered around the city, as well as pools in the YMCA, Montreal High School and the MAAA.

But there's no beach.

The Low Down on Night Life

THERE ARE SEVERAL GARAGES IN THE UPTOWN AREA where you can store your car for any reasonable length of time. It is wise to do so because Montreal's traffic is so tangled it's practically snarled. Don't leave any valuables in the car while it's parked on the street. It's an even-money bet that they won't be there when you come back.

IN OTHER CITIES YOU CAN TELL IF A CAB IS VACANT BY the roof light. If it's out, the cab is occupied; if it's on the cab is for hire. But not in Montreal. So many hackies disregard the signal that you can never tell whether or not it's available. There are some four thousand cabs roaming around the town but you can't find one on a rainy day. Best bet is to telephone for one and let the dispatcher worry. The fare is undergoing a boost to a thirty-five cent drop—but it's still the best and the cheapest way to travel if you are going from spot to spot in the city.

CLIP JOINTS ARE RARE IN MONTREAL AND EVEN IF YOU want to find one you'll be in for a hard time. However, some waiters will give you the big deal if you're not careful. If this happens, call the headwaiter or the manager. But—a word to the wise. Check up on the prices and be sure you're right before beefing.

THERE ARE VERY FEW SPEAKEASIES IN MONTREAL. THE competition from legitimate night spots is too tough to make them profitable. However, if you must do your drinking illegally, you'll find one on Drummond near Osborne [which became Lagauchetière] and the odd one here and there. Ask a cab driver. The prices, you'll discover, are jacked way up and it just isn't worth it.

YOU CAN BUY A BOTTLE OF LIQUOR WITHOUT GIVING your name and address at any of the numerous Quebec Liquor Commission stores. You won't need a license (Torontonians—eat your hearts out) nor are you rationed. There is more personal freedom in Quebec than in any other province and your right to drink what and when you please has been safeguarded by the sanest set of liquor laws in the Dominion. Q.L.C. outlets do not usually sell beer. This you order from your grocer, either in quarts or pints. Rare ales from England may be obtained from the liquor stores.

DON'T TRY TO SMUGGLE A DOLL UP TO YOUR HOTEL ROOM without first making a deal with the staff. Montreal house detectives are a competent lot. They know all the answers—they've heard all the questions. A fin proffered in a discreet manner may get you under the wire, but don't bank on it.

IF YOU WEAR A HAT, CHECK IT. IN THE WINTER YOU WILL be forced to wear a top coat—check that too. Although a few places have compulsory checking charges, no spot is going to let you in unless you park your hat and coat with the hat check girl. The gals don't keep this money for themselves but turn it over to the concessionaire. Most manage to steal a few bucks per week to augment their salary. There is a new trend toward non-tipping currently the vogue in town. For instance, the Laurentien Hotel forbids the practice, as does the Indian Room. At either of these places you'll see signs asking you not to tip—so don't. You'll only embarrass the girl and it may cost her her job if she accepts.

THE LEGAL CURFEW HOUR IN MONTREAL IS TWO AYEM— but don't pay too much attention to it. Most spots stay open till the last customer has left. Every now and then a crusade rears his ugly head and all night spots are closed up at the appointed hour. But these crusades never last long and even when they do, there are always the odd spots that cheat on the deal. There is only one day in Montreal when you can't get a drink before midnight. That is Good Friday. All spots, by mutual agreement, close their doors.

Even if your blood brother owns a nitery, don't ask him to serve you a drink before midnight. He'll risk losing his license if he does.

IF IT IS AT ALL POSSIBLE, DON'T GO OUT ON SATURDAY night. That is the night when all niteries are jampacked by those of the lesser income brackets. Café Society usually remains at home and house parties are the gathering spots of those who would normally be ringsiding it. Saturday night is the one night the shoe clerks can go out and howl. And it is an unwritten law that those who club around every other night move over and give them room. Niteries usually stage an additional show on Saturdays so that those who can't afford to dawdle—at those prices—may have the opportunity of seeing same without hocking the furniture.

GET TO KNOW YOUR LOCAL BARTENDER. THIS IS MOST important. Local mixologists are good people to know in an emergency. They can get you anything you want at any time of the day and night and will do so, providing they know you.

Besides, if you are alone in the bar it is always nice to have someone to talk to.

Tale of Two Cities

IF YOU ARE HAVING DINNER with a group of Montrealers and suddenly bring up the subject of Toronto, chances are that one will remark, "Toronto? Please. Not while I'm eating."

The feud between Canada's two major cities is actually a one-sided affair. For, although Montrealers despise Torontonians, the feeling is not mutual. We have yet to hear a citizen of the Queen City cast disparaging remarks about Montreal, with the exception of a few who have decided that too many French-Canadians live there.

The resentment Montrealers feel toward Torontonians is by no means groundless. Citizens from the Ontario capital descend en masse to Montreal and a few, not the majority mind you, make themselves sufficiently obnoxious as to create an inhospitable feeling in a town where hospitality is everyone's stock-in-trade.

For instance: One night we were holding down our usual section of El Morocco's bar when a well-dressed individual sidled up to us and parked his elbow next to ours. He immediately engaged us in conversation, and, in no time whatsoever, we learned that he had built up a business from nothing to the half-million dollar class.

We told him that we were very happy to hear about this example of Canadian industry and, as a natural gesture, ordered him a drink. He told us he was from

Toronto and was on a selling trip to Montreal and that he had a suite at the Mount Royal and that life was very good indeed.

He told us he liked Montreal very much and was very interested in the colorful history of the town. We bought him another drink.

He went on to say that he was amazed that an English-speaking young man like myself could live among so many French-Canadians. Then we stopped buying him drinks. For a moment we wondered if we could have him heaved down the stairs but, instead, simply marked it off as crass ignorance.

Disregarding our sudden coolness, he ventured that drinks were very expensive in the club. With the deepest sarcasm we could muster, we informed him that the floor show cost something like $8,000 per week and where did he think he was—in some Bay Street beverage room?

Came then a very boring monologue having to do with how much his firm had made during the past year and how much it expected to make in the following year—but no offer of a drink. This went on until he called—in a very loud voice—for his check. He went over it like a lost mariner searching for land and then proffered a $50 bill. There was eight cents among his change and that was what he left his bartender.

This, of course, is probably an isolated example. But, unfortunately, Torontonians have a name for being slow men with a buck. Headwaiters manage to crowd them into the most remote places of a night club. Bartenders serve them only after everyone else has been taken care of. Too many Queen City characters are noisy. Too many complain too frequently that the price of drinks is too high. And too many get the idea that Montreal is one big playground where, if they have enough money, they can do whatever they please.

These types are tolerated. After all, they do no great harm to the town. But there are others who do not appreciate that Montreal is a French city. Give them one week in the town and they want everybody should speak English.

Although not necessarily penny pinchers, they are reluctant to leave an adequate tip. They give waiters, waitresses and bartenders a superior glance (which impresses no one) and resent having to leave gratuities for service which they consider is rightfully theirs and included in the tab.

Now that they are building a subway in their town, the airs will, no doubt, become more superior. They will gaze down—as if from a great height—upon the lowly Montrealer, and, if not blocked in the beginning, there will be no living with them.

True, Toronto is a far more aggressive town than Montreal. There is more money speculated on Bay Street than there is on St. James. True, more Torontonians own their homes than do Montrealers, and all agree that their taxes are lower than ours.

Their street car service is cheaper and better. Their motormen and conductors are more polite. Their policemen are more co-operative and have been known to even smile sometimes. They own more cars and drive far better than do us Quebeckers. Their wages are higher and their cost of living is lower. They have less poverty, finer buildings, more money and a beautiful lake.

They have more and better homes, a better China-town, bigger and better theaters, more industries, a better hockey team, wider streets, cheaper cigarettes, more tele-phones and we could go on and on.

But if you think we are the type who would naturally say, "We wouldn't live there if you gave us the place," we have a surprise for you.

We'd live there if you gave us the place—but under no other condition.

Montreal and Toronto are not merely two different cities. They are two different worlds.

Hi, Shport!

MONTREAL'S FAVORITE SPORT—outdoor type, that is, is hockey. No other game even comes close to it in popularity and interest. Some claim the game was invented in Montreal but this has been denied by many who say it was first played in Kingston, Ontario.

At present there is only one National Hockey League entry, Les Canadiens, pronounced "Lay Canayen," representing Montreal. There were two at one time. The Maroons, made up mostly of English-speaking players, and Les Canadiens who were, in the main, French.

When the two teams met it, was the signal for some of the greatest free-for-alls ever to be staged in the Forum. Today you can get a good idea of what it was like by watching a team match at the wrestling bouts.

Back during the two-team era, you had to support either one or the other of the teams. Being neutral was not allowed. It was customary to line up outside the Forum at two in the afternoon and wait in the snow until game time at eight-thirty. You paid a half-dollar for this privilege—unless, of course, you were in the upper brackets and could afford a reserved seat.

Les Canadiens had the most rabid supporters. They were known as "The Millionaires" and had a club of their own on St. Kit's east. The club later became The Versailles and featured strip tease artists rather than hockey fans.

The Millionaires would show up at the Rush End—the north section of the rink—wearing the familiar red, white and blue sweaters and would create a riot before game time. Seems as though the favorite stunt was to tear up newspapers, magazines, etc., into tiny pieces, and to throw them in the air as their idols came out on the ice.

It was an unwritten law that Canadiens supporters occupied the western half of the Rush End while Maroon supporters sat in the eastern half. This also served the purpose of dividing the two factions and also making it easier for one to know who his enemies were during the frequent fisticuffs.

Back in those days Howie Morenz starred for Les Canadiens. He is still regarded as being the greatest hockey player ever to don skates. His unfortunate death was a great blow to the game and he was mourned by Canadiens and Maroon supporters alike.

Other Habitants around at that time were the Mantha brothers, Johnny Gagnon, Araman Mondou, Albert Leduc, Pit Lepine, Aurel Joliat, Armand Raymond, Art Alexandre, George Hainsworth and Art Lesieur.

Most of them are still around. Leduc is a big hotel man in nearby Valleyfield. Armand Raymond operated Le Coq d'Or during the war and later opened the Zanzibar in the East End. At present he is running a lodge in the Laurentians.

Idol for the Maroon supporters was Nels "Old Poison" Stewart. Big Nels had every goalie in the league developing ulcers. He had a murderous shot and a sharp eye for an unprotected corner. His running mate was

Hooley Smith. Smith later opened a billiard parlor on St. Kit's. He is still running it if we're not mistaken.

Other stars of that time were Marty Burke, Red Dutton, Jimmy Ward, Kave Kerr and Flat Walsh. Dutton went on to become a millionaire in the contracting business. For a time, he headed the NHL board of directors.

Boxing draws a good crowd whether held at the Forum or at the ball park. There is more betting on boxing than on any other sport locally.

Next to hockey the greatest box office attraction is wrestling. This is due to Eddie Quinn who came up from Boston just before the war to take over the promotion end of the game. Quinn raised the sport, just before it gave its last dying gasp, into the top-flight box-office brackets.

He brought in such names as Jack Dempsey and Jack Sharkey to referee. Booked such grapplers as Primo Carnera, Gorgeous George, Ski Hi Lee, Mike Mazurki and Larry Moquin. Star of the stable, of course, is French Canadian Yvon Robert.

Robert, apart from being the biggest drawing card, is also a successful restaurant operator. He owns Au Petit Robinson in Ile Bizard, where your table is set up in the trees and a few Tarzan-like waiters climb up to serve you.

He also operates, along with his brothers, La Bohéme on Guy Street just opposite. His Majesty's Theatre. La Bohème was once a famous joint before it became a night club. Many had tried to operate it successfully before Robert took over. It is a great afternoon gathering spot.

Snowshoeing, once a popular sport here, is dying

out. On the other hand, curling is becoming more popular. The "roaring game" is said to have been first played here back in 1759 by members of Wolfe's army at Quebec.

Golf is becoming more popular and there are a few top rate courses within driving distance of the city. At one time Fletcher's Field was a golf course and many old timers still remember batting the ball around the area.

Montrealers have been racing fans from way back. In 1871 the original Blue Bonnets track opened on Lower Lachine Road near Montreal West. Close by the old Belair Track owned by J.P. Dawes. There was another track running in the eastern section of the city called the Lepine Course.

The bangtails business was in its glory when the present Blue Bonnet track opened in 1907. Since then, many tracks have come and gone. The old Delorimier track opened in 1914 for flat racing; King Edward Park was operating about the same time as was Kempton Park in Laprairie.

Two other circuits, Dorval and Mount Royal, opened and closed after many years of successful racing. Dorval was torn down to make room for the airport. Delorimier was torn down to make way for a housing development. Only Blue Bonnets operates at present.

Canadian football, which originated from English rugby and developed into the American-style mayhem, got its biggest boost when the Alouettes were organized a few years ago.

Chiefly responsible for bringing the game up to major-league status is Leo Dandurand, who imported

Coach Lew Heyman to master-mind the mastodons. The Alouettes play at the Ball Park and draw a heavy crowd.

Most surprising thing about the Alouettes is that they draw the French-Canadians out to see a game which the Habitants have ignored for years. It may be that the name was wisely chosen, but it's more probably that the type of football played appeals to the French.

Swing Street

NO ONE SEEMS TO REMEMBER where Stanley Street picked up the name of Swing Street. There are only four night clubs on the stretch and none feature hot music.

Oldest established club on the strip is the Hawaiian Lounge. At time of writing, the spot is closed with license troubles. At one time it was the Stanley Grill—one of the plushier spas to operate in the city.

The Stanley had the best shows and the finest music. Joe Nito's orchestra backed up top name acts and it was the thing to do to wind up at The Stanley.

Many times the roof was open during a sudden rain and everyone complained of being served watered liquor. The removable ceiling is no longer in operation and the spacious dance floor now holds a circular bar.

Resident act at the Hawaiian is the Irving Paul collection of half-demented musicians and actors. Paul, who sports a spade beard, heads what was the zaniest show in the city. You're likely to hear everything from a hammed-up Rigoletto to some jivey jazz. Anything is likely to happen—and usually does.

Downstairs from the Hawaiian is the Tic-Toc, which is also closed at time of writing. It was formerly the Lido, another of the city's original plushy spots. The Lido's lounge featured built-in pinball machines in its tables.

There is some talk that it will reopen soon with a balcony, chorus and big name acts. Before it closed, it

Ad, *The Montreal Standard*, April 16, 1949.
Meilan Lam fonds, Concordia University Archives, P135

had one of the longest bars in the city. The longest is the
one at Au Faisan Doré.

A few doors south of The Lido is the Esquire, which
holds some sort of record for continuous operation as a
night club. The Esky is owned by Sammy Cleaver who
also has a slice of Chez Maurice.

The Esquire was noted for its floor shows and its top
ranking waiter, King Pete Wyman. King Pete served the
suds at the spot for so many years the place looked empty
when he left, just after the war, to open a theatrical
rooming house.

The Esquire survived the loss, however, and still runs without the usual chorus. If you go in for smorgasbord, you'll find a table near the entrance loaded with the stuff.

North of St. Kit's on Stanley Street is the Gumbo Cafe, formerly the Nightcap. During the war and a few years following, it had the reputation of being the roughest, toughest drinking house in the city.

The spot was run by Johnny "The Wop" Pannunzio who also bought into the Zanzibar. Johnny was a sick man for several years before he died. He was also one of the biggest-hearted guys around the town.

No returned soldier ever had to go without a buck as long as The Wop was around. His place used to open and close and open and close. It was a favorite target of Pax Plante who wanted to keep the spot closed permanently.

Following Pannunzio's death, the place changed hands. It lost a lot of lustiness, although it was one of the dozen to lose its license during the recent campaign. It is now a more gentle place to visit.

Shot in the Arm, Bud?

MONTREAL'S DOPE PEDDLING center is the corner of Clark and St. Kit's. Many efforts have been made to wipe the scourge off the map in Montreal but so far every effort has failed.

The biggest scare the junkies ever got came from the weekly newspaper, *The Standard*, when Ken Johnstone, one of the town's ablest reporters, and his photographer, Louis Jacques, rented a cheap room in a run-down flophouse near the corner and watched the peddler come and go for some time.

Jacques kept his camera trained on the sellers while Johnstone disguised himself as an addict and made contacts. He reported he had found little trouble buying the stuff that dreams are made of, and his story, along with Jacques' pictures, scared the hell out of the corner for weeks.

Local policemen are hampered in their work because they are known to both peddlers and users. As soon as a cop comes near the area, the junkies make themselves scarce. Police everywhere have little use for dopies—they are held in less esteem than even stoolies and pimps.

Therefore, when one gets tangled with the law, he can expect little mercy. The big boys of the racket are the out-of-towners. The Montreal flow for years originated in Vancouver and has been channeled into Montreal through various routes and by various methods.

Although Montreal is a seaport, little of the stuff arrives through this entrance. The RCMP has the traffic down to a minimum and have, on several occasions, confiscated quantities of narcotics before they reached the dock.

The general belief that most opium smokers are Orientals is strictly a pipe dream. They are not. There is little trade in narcotics around Chinatown—although there is the odd addict.

Most local snowbirds favour cocaine. Actually, this drug, like marijuana, is not habit-forming to any great degree. Morphine, like cocaine, comes from opium. Morphine is not listed as being habit-forming either.

Getting known is not too difficult a problem. Just hang around for a few hours and, chances are, you'll find yourself in conversation with some stranger who will suggest a friendly cup of coffee.

The stranger will expect you to bring up the subject of getting a supply. Once the niceties of conversation lag, he will disappear and a colleague will deliver the stuff to you.

Marijuana is not as popular among teenagers as it is in other large cities. Strict policing has cleared most of the sellers away from their favorite selling spots near the schools, but you can still buy the drug on Antoine Street.

One of the disadvantages of marijuana is its odor— it smells like boiled tea, hence the tag "tea." Before a "tea party" can get under way, windows, doors and even keyholes must be plugged to keep the smoke from escaping. Any house detective with a nose in working order can spot the stuff almost immediately.

Sentimental—Oui!

So that is Montreal—the gaudy, bawdy settlement on the St. Lawrence. It is not so much a city as a state of mind. To live there is to love it. Those of us who were fortunate to be born there consider it the nearest approach to Heaven we know of without leaving the ground.

Montreal is many things. It is the sun sinking over the Town of Mount Royal and rising from the Harbor Bridge. It is stealing lumps of sugar from the Chick-N-Coop and the Laurentien Restaurant and feeding them to the horses outside the Pure Milk Stable on Dorchester Street.

It is the sense of personal freedom and the lack of blue laws, which permit you to live normally without Mother Grundies giving you a hard time. It is eating peanuts at the ball park during a Sunday double header.

It is sitting around Slitkins on fight night discussing the fight business with Butch Obie. It is being invited to Tony the Tailor's for a spaghetti dinner. It is showing off your gal at Ruby Foo's. It is the finale at the Bellevue Casino.

It is talking about Canadianism with Tony, the German-born waiter at the Pine Lounge, and it is saying "hello" to Bob the headwaiter at the Folies Bergères. It is mingling with the guests at Joe Margolis' Sunday afternoon parties and it is whistling at Lili St. Cyr.

Trumpeter Bix Belair's big band at the Auditorium,
Montreal, probably 1940s.
*Photo: Marcel Deschamps. John Gilmore fonds,
Concordia University Archives, P004-02-107*

It is the calm peacefulness of Mount Royal on a summer's night and the blaring noise of Peel and St. Kit's. It is following a seven with an eleven at a crap game, and picking two winners in a row at Blue Bonnets.

Montreal is many things. It is gagging with the owners of Churchill's Drug Store and it is listening to the words of wisdom of Père Racine of La Ligue de Sacré-Cœur. It is the apostles atop St. James Basilica and the quiet dignity of Notre Dame on Place d'Armes.

It is Germaine Giroux singing a French torch song. It is Antoinette Giroux saying a thousand words with a typical Gallic shrug of her shoulders. It is Bix Belair playing "La Vie en Rose" and Max Chamitov playing a Viennese waltz.

It is Ferdinand Racicot's fascinating French accent when he speaks English and Lorne Clarke's fascinating English accent when he speaks French. It is Marcel's savoir faire when he serves you at Le Pigalle and the deep bow with which Victor greets you on the Normandie Roof.

It is the morning parade of the bellboys at the Laurentien Hotel and Harry Miller's cheery greeting at the Corso Pizzeria. It is Frankie D'Asti's ability to make you at home at the Hi-Ho and Slitkin's and Slotkin's mangled English.

It is the midnight show at the Gayety Theatre and the Sunday afternoon jam sessions at the Café St. Michel. It is the first snowfall; it is the breath-taking beauty of the morning sun on Fletcher's Field.

Montreal is many things and it would take a Shakespeare to capture, in words, the magic of the city...and we are no Shakespeare. That's for sure.

Handy Reference

Bellevue Casino
Ontario near Bleury. Big shows, pretty girls. Admission is one buck Thursday through Saturday. Half buck other days.

Aldo's
Mountain near Dorchester. Wind-up spot. Good food. No dancing. Music.

Chez Maurice
St. Kit's near Mountain. Soon to open as a cabaret with show and steaks.

Folies Bergéres
St. Lawrence below St. Kit's. Admission one buck. Big shows, chorus and dancing.

Jamaica Grill
Mountain near Dorchester. Charcoal-broiled steaks. No dancing. Piano music. Upstairs features Gay Nineties Room with Adelaide Cook and Doc Reid. You can sing to your heart's content and get piano accompaniment, already.

Flamingo
Drummond Street above Dorchester. Straight drinking and eating spot with the accent on chrome and red leather.

THE YACHT CLUB
Drummond and St. Kit's. One of the secluded, quiet and dimly lit spots where conversation is carried on in whispers. No show, no dancing and no music. If your nerves are on edge and you want to relax—this is the spot to do it. It has a marine décor and the drinks are extraordinarily good.

THE 400 CLUB
Drummond near Sherbrooke. Formerly the gathering place of the Blue Bloods, this spot is now just an eating and drinking house. The society crowd don't go there in as great a number as they did but the food is still good and the atmosphere is quiet.

SLITKINS AND SLOTKINS
Dorchester near Mountain. Good food. No dancing. Still the place to go upon arrival in the city. Fight fans make this their headquarters.

MONTREAL PRESS CLUB
Laurentien Hotel. Unless you're a member, you must find a member to bring you in. There is a special night set aside when females are permitted to enter its sacred portals. Drinks are cheaper here but you can't pay for them unless you hold a membership card. So make certain your escort has loot with him because he'll have to pay the tab. Nice set-up, huh?

PINE LOUNGE
Laurentian Hotel. If you want to make an impression on your date meet her here. The room has a distinct northern flavor and the staff is one of the most competent in town.

The Normandie Roof atop the Mount Royal Hotel, 1937.
Joe Bell scrapbook, Concordia University Archives, 2.p3a.

NORMANDIE ROOF
Mount Royal Hotel. Take your American guest here and automatically stop him from boasting about the beautiful night clubs back home. This is one of the most lavish rooms on the continent. Entertainment is good and there is dancing. Food is tops. Victor is the maitre d'.

CAFE DE L'EST
Notre Dame Street east: This spot is a long way from Peel and St. Kit's but it is worth the drive if you care for Parisian type shows. The place is a rambling mansion with several bars dotted here and there about the spot.

THE BEL-A
St. Kit's near Drummond. This is the favourite hangout

of waiters and waitresses. Tony and Gus were the waiters there at one time and may still be there.

THE DRUMMOND CAFÉ
Drummond Street. Formerly the Drumhurst, this spot was once the rendezvous of the mining crowd. Now it attracts the younger set. If you're looking for an old army buddy—try here first.

THE INDIAN ROOM
St. Kit's near Drummond. Favorite with afternoon shoppers. Food is terrific. No dancing.

THE MELODY
Sherbrooke near Jeanne Mance. Favorite spa of French professional men. The guy next to you may be famous. The club attracts those on the border of the arty crowd.

LA TOUR EIFFEL
Stanley near St. Kit's. A choice eating spot if you like French cooking—and who doesn't? The arty crowd congregate here—writers, painters and poets.

Index

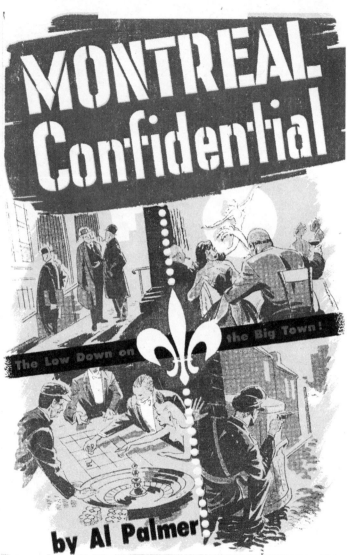

Original front cover, 1950

Montreal Confidential

by AL PALMER

Our Old Man used to always say that you can take the boy out of Montreal but you can't take Montreal out of the boy.

Some cities are merely blots on the landscape with the approved collection of steel and stone buildings and the ever-present supermarkets. Most have absolutely nothing to distinguish them from a thousand similar cities.

Some, notably New York, New Orleans and San Francisco, have certain characteristics which set them apart from the other cities.

And then there's Montreal.

There is little doubt but that our home town has developed into the most colorful community on the continent. Nothing which New York, New Orleans or San Francisco—or any other city for that matter—can offer that Montreal hasn't more of.

It is a helluva town to visit, a helluva town to live in and a helluva town to come back to. We love every grimy square foot of it.

A NEWS STAND LIBARY POCKET EDITION

Original back cover, 1950